D1548606

LITTLE BLACK BOOK

– for moms –

SOFIE VALKIERS

LITTLE BLACK BOOK

—for moms—

from pregnancy
to the first year of life

PHOTOGRAPHY BY
MARCIO BASTOS

LANNOO

Content

PART II – HE'S HERE!
And there he is: our little Gabriel bastos! – p. 82

FROM GIRL BO$$ TO MOMMY BO$$

Paris, October, 5th 2016. Got up extra early to prep for the Louis Vuitton show, the very last major show of this Paris Fashion Week. It promises to be a busy day, delightfully chaotic, with editorial & street style shoots, outfit swaps, meetings, the show, writing interviews and quick reports, and a big party to finish off. And here we are sitting in our hotel room, my boyfriend Marcio and I – both of us still in bathrobes, **staring at the pregnancy test in complete disbelief**. Is this for real??

And that's how the arrival of our first tiny baby announced itself: amidst the chaos of our always-on-the-road lives, in the world's biggest fashion capital where we had first met 10 years ago, right in between the fashion shows. Looking back, it feels pretty symbolic to me: **the baby was right smack-bang in the middle of the life we loved to lead**, just as we had always wanted. I glanced from the test to the show invitation; an invitation from Louis Vuitton next to an invitation to become parents – it was so us! :)

Us becoming parents, there couldn't be a more surreal concept. With a Brazilian boyfriend whose family is everything to him, and the close ties I have to my own family, we were simply dying to have a little brother or sister for our fat grey tomcat, Bobke. It wasn't until our trip to Thailand, where we celebrated our 10th anniversary together, that we starting seeing things in more tangible terms, and a few months later we had that specific day in Paris when everything suddenly became very, very real. :)

Making a tiny person and including him in your life: it sounds fantastic and scary and overwhelming... and 1001 other things that all went through my mind at once while I reapplied my mascara one last time and got into the taxi to one of my favourite designer shows – ready, set, go! And that neatly summarises the biggest challenge I faced in being pregnant:

my intuition has always been my most important guiding light (who remembers my second book? ;)), both personally and professionally. And as these things go, at the same time I'm also a serious control freak who wants to get a grip on everything and decide the funnest way to do things. It just gives me a sense of peace and the room to be free and creative. And then there's suddenly a baby. :) How do you fit a tiny new person with his own personality and (literally) loud voice into the busy life that you secretly adore, and that you worked really hard to achieve? That's something that pretty much every career woman (and man!) faces at some point: **how do you combine *girl bo$$* with *mama bo$$* without feeling like you're not doing it right?**

I've gotten a lot of practical questions, and when I did a bit of research myself to prepare for the arrival of our own baby, I quickly saw why: there simply aren't a lot of people offering practical tips on where to find the most stylish maternity clothes (they're out there, I promise!), how to do deal with a difficult pregnancy (still so taboo!), which products are best for the baby's nursery (expect my official statement against fluo toys), which yummy snacks are really best for you and your baby, which secret beauty tricks can magically erase the effects of short nights, and the best way to handle a loooooong flight with you plus your mini. That and more is exactly what you'll find in this book: **my most personal story ever, straight from the heart, and stuffed with tangible tips for making this new part of your life as fabulous as possible.** Ready, set, go!

SOFIE

VALKIERS

BEFORE

PART ONE

BABY

I'll admit freely: when we first realised that we were having a baby, that day in Paris, we had zero idea of what we could expect. That's just how Marcio and I were living our lives: making the most of whatever crossed our path, without anticipating and planning the whole time. Some part of me just automatically assumed that a baby would work the same way; **we'd just see what happened and keep leading our normal lives in the meantime**.

O BABY BABY: MAXI PREP FOR YOUR MINI

It's almost funny when I look back on it, because the reality was pretty much exactly the opposite: from morning sickness that lasted 24/7 for weeks, those first ultrasound images that envelop you in soooo much love and other emotions, putting together your baby's wardrobe and nursery room, and of course dealing with your constantly changing body... Yup, the list of things you have to prepare for your mini is mega-maxi, and takes a whole lot of patience, a series of sleepless nights, and even more daydreaming about what's going to happen next. One thing's for sure: **you're only pregnant with your first baby once, so – chaos or not – try to keep that in mind**. For everything else, you'll find your ultimate checklist here, so you can make it through those 9 unique months in style and (relative) calm!

Fashion

It's such a familiar feeling. Yes, you're unbelievably happy to be pregnant, and yes, you can't wait to actually meet your little baby, but **yikes, what a super scary thought: your entire body's going to change!** It might sound shallow, but guess what? I love my wardrobe. A lot. :) The idea that I might have to say a temporary farewell to my favourite pieces and exchange them for ones that would fit over my big, round belly did not seem appealing to me, to say the least. And especially not when I was confronted with what passes for standard maternity fashion – not good. Until I realised something: **this is the perfect opportunity to dust off my most creative styling tips!** And it turned out to be surprisingly fun, because when it was finally time to say goodbye to my baby bump, I actually got a little emotional (sigh, just typical!). So if you're asking yourself what kind of outfits you can find to wear during these 9 months to take you stylishly through grocery shopping **(practical)**, meetings **(sophisticated)**, hangouts with your besties **(fun)**, and dates with your baby daddy **(sexy),** you can be sure that there's a **matching, on-trend, baby-bump outfit for every occasion!**

DRESS THE BUMP
1-3 MONTHS: HIDE & SEEK

THE STYLING

For the first 3 months, I didn't notice my baby bump that much. Instead of gaining a little weight (at 3 months, your baby is about the size of a lime), I lost a few kilos thanks to the constant nausea (more on that later!). On top of that, like so many mamas-to-be, I still wanted to **keep my pregnancy a bit hidden** during those risky first months, so comfy, feel-good pieces and my more form-fitting favourite clothing that wouldn't fit me any more in just a bit: those became my go-to items.

TIP 1 // AVOID MATERNITY CLOTHES

It may sound like a no-brainer, but if you don't want to look pregnant in the first few months, avoid maternity clothes as much as you can. And I'll take it a step further – wear the clothing you'll soon have to say goodbye to every chance you get! Now's the time to wear all your denim in your fav **denim-on-denim combos**. And yes, you can take that very literally: go ahead and pair your favourite denim shirt with jeans, with or without the same wash (that's the great thing about denim: everything can go with every occasion), and add some sneakers and a hot jacket for the perfect badass outfit! Oh, and if your jeans are already getting a little tight, then try the **elastic band trick**: thread a hair tie through the buttonhole and wrap it around the button to buy yourself a couple extra centimetres. It's that easy!

TIP 2 // DRAW ATTENTION AWAY FROM YOUR BELLY

There's no better way to keep your mini-bump hidden than to shift the emphasis to another part of your body. And that's easy to do with **striking accessories or details that are just a little bit different**! Despite the fact that my first trimester was in winter, I was often spotted in my favourite tasselled blouse, choker necklace with maxi charms, oversized smiley-face bag, and playful monster-print sneakers. In short, lots of small details that make you smile and divert attention from your belly! **Start with a simple basic piece**, like always-flattering wide trousers in a neutral colour, such as dark blue, and **match** to your heart's content **with the craziest pieces in your closet**.

TIP 3 // BREAK UP YOUR SILHOUETTE

Contrary to popular belief, a dark monochrome outfit (dark blue, brown, or black) does not necessarily camouflage things. Colourful prints are a much better idea, and they also make your complexion look better! If you're not a big fan of prints and prefer monochrome, then go for **bright monochro-**

matic colours, which you can pair with each other in unexpected ways. Orange + red or hot pink? Purple + red or pink? As long as you don't pick super tight items, there's a good chance that the effect will be loads of fun.

TIP 4 // LAYERS AND OVERSIZED!

And if your belly is really hard to hide, there are always layers and oversized items! Loose-fitting slip dresses over a top or a casual sporty ensemble with a wide sweatshirt – all super stylish and wonderfully comfy. Or if you need to dress it up a little more, try a pair of over-the-knee velvet boots with a trench coat! Sexy and chic – always. And however difficult it may be: **keep your hand off your belly as much as possible**, because no outfit can hide that reflex! ;)

THE SHOPS

BASICS / LEVI'S (MEN)

If you already have a little belly but you still don't feel like jumping into maternity denim straight away, take a peek at the Levi's **men's collection**! The **classic low rise 501s and 511s** pair perfectly with kitten heels and a cool jacket. And that relaxed tomboy vibe is a free bonus!

COMFORT / COS

COS has a specific leisurewear collection that's extra comfy, and pretty much the whole collection is absolutely perfect for a growing belly. And with a colour scheme that focuses on **earth tones** (white, black, nude, brick red, salmon pink), you can go wild with your acces-sories; you'll always, always, always keep fitting into those. ;)

TRENDS / HATCH

One of the most annoying features of mater-nity wear is, of course, the idea that you have to invest in something that you'll only wear for a really short time. Hatch, an American brand (they offer international shipping!), is here to help, with a very extensive collection that's **also perfect if you're not pregnant** – think casual pantsuits, oversized stripy sweaters, flattering caftans, and even a limited edition swimsuit line, all in timeless prints and on-trend colours. They also often launch amazing collections with specialised designers like Current/Elliott (ready-to-wear), Bandier (workout), and Marysia (swimwear)!

DRESS THE BUMP
4-6 MONTHS: IS SHE...?

THE STYLING

My second trimester: hallelujah!! At month 4, the nausea started to fade and my baby bump was finally starting to show (around 6 months, your baby's about the size of a melon). So it's about time to show off that beautiful belly, so you'll avoid those "Is she...?" questions as much as possible. Yes, she is! :)

TIP 1 // LEGGINGS, BABY!

Leggings: they really are saviours in this no-more-jeans phase! The only problem? They look so boring so quickly! My favourite way to add a bit of gangster to my leggings is adding a cropped bomber jacket in camouflage print. **The shorter cut means your belly is still visible and the print**, in neutral shades of khaki and brown, **has a super cool effect** when combined with an all-black outfit.

TIP 2 // AN ODE TO THE PENCIL SKIRT

The biggest challenge in the second trimester is finding a way to highlight your tummy in a sophisticated way (so without going too crazy with tight items that can be a bit tacky). A knee-length pencil skirt is perfect for this, especially **paired with a classic striped shirt and T-shirt with playful text – all to give your look more punch**. Add in a pair of sexy patent leather ankle boots, *et voilà*!

TIP 3 // MIX & MATCH TEXTURES

One of my favourite ways to make an outfit just that little bit different is **mixing contrasting materials** (light and delicate + heavy and rough)! Wide, loose-fitting trousers with a satin sheen (and a stretchy band at the top, of course!) plus a cashmere V-neck halter and XXL suede jacket: yes and yes! **Give the sweater more of a waistline by tucking it loosely into the trousers**, and finish it with your favourite pair of chunky sneakers and a big shopper bag.

TIP 4 // CINCH LIKE A PRO

It may not be for everyone, but for me it was an amazing way to make my belly look great in an oversized striped shirt: just add a bustier top! Pick one that's suitable for the purpose, meaning **beautifully finished, made from rich fabrics** (velvet is perfect) **and in a sophisticated colour pattern** (pink: nope; black or brick red: yes). Pair with form-fitting leggings to balance out your wider top half nicely!

THE SHOPS

BASICS / JOSEPH

If you're looking for the softest, high-quality wool sweaters and tops (and matching pencil skirts!), then Joseph is definitely the brand for you. They have a super pretty **knitwear collection with masses of basics in neutral shades, plus a few more experimental items** – fringes on the sleeves or a special texture, if you're looking for a little extra.

COMFORT / BLANQI

While some of my girlfriends struggled with swollen hands and feet, skin problems, or hair loss (eek!), my biggest problem was my growing belly. I naturally have a pretty slim waist, and it was so crazy to suddenly feel the extra weight there! It's a sure way to develop back problems (even at night), so Blanqi's supportive collection really came in handy. The **seamless shirts and leggings** are designed to **give extra support** in the places that carry the most extra weight as your bump grows, and they **look perfect under a form-fitting dress** (great for parties!).

TRENDS / A PEA IN THE POD

This online store has a nice selection of maternity clothes from 'regular' brands like Splendid and 7 for All Mankind or Paige jeans (also one of my personal favs!). You can easily find **more on-trend pieces** with cool prints, like a camo tracksuit or stretchy pencil skirt.

DRESS THE BUMP
6-9 MONTHS: BIG & BEAUTIFUL

THE STYLING

Aaaah the 3rd trimester: time to bring out your very best styling tricks, because believe me: every time you think your belly is as big as it's going to get, it gets a bit bigger (and at the end of it all, your baby will be ready to make a grand entrance!). And the mission is this: **to make everything that still fits around your belly look elegant, stylish, and not too girly!**

TIP 1 // RIBBON BELT TRICK

The most important accessory at this point in your pregnancy? A belt! Pick one that you **can tie yourself so it can grow along with your belly,** and use it to cinch your dresses and tops just above your baby bump. To keep your ribbon belt from looking too cutesy (especially paired with your belly), all you need to do is **add a few edgy details**: fur-accented slip-ons, a big black bag (to balance out your bump a bit :)) and oversized earrings.

TIP 2 // GIRL POWER SUIT

A two-piece suit for women is something that will always be stylish and powerful, with or without a bump. Something in a **flowing material like silk** feels wonderful on the baby bump (don't forget to cinch the waistline with the matching ribbon, see above!), and if you have the option, go for **vertical stripes to slim down your silhouette** – for those days that you just want to feel normal again. Pair it with pointy flats (which have the same effect, by the way), because heels *definitely* aren't third-trimester material.

TIP 3 // ANIMAL PRINTS

Yep, it's possible to wear cool outfits during those final months, and you'll do it with the help of... animal prints! It's something that many people – pregnant or not – seem to be struggling with, but I think it's the perfect way to give your outfit that little extra something. How do you make sure it doesn't come across as tacky? Pick **a piece that doesn't immediately dominate your whole look** (a simple shirt is perfect), and combine it with some 'safer' options like a knitted midi dress (**staying below the knee is crucial!**), flat moccasins and a slouchy black bag.

TIP 4 // THE MAXI DRESS

You saw it coming: the flowy maxi dress is the big hero of the third trimester. In fact, it's just about the only thing I could still fit into during the last couple weeks. And the biggest advantage is that you can **keep wearing it after your pregnancy**. Pick a **nice flowing fabric** that falls loosely around your bump. An **irregular hem** or **knee-high split** always adds a sexy note. Finish with serious, glamorous accents like pumps with a chunky transparent heel or low-slung mules (stilettos certainly won't be among your favourite footwear now ;)) and a gold cuff bracelet.

TIP 5 // BORROW FROM YOUR BOYFRIEND

Not interested in traditional maternity clothes? No problem, because clothes that can accommodate a round belly may be closer than you think: in your baby daddy's closet! :) **I regularly went shopping in Marcio's wardrobe** for a pair of slouchy jeans or relaxed shirt that would fit around my belly. Don't forget to add some feminine details, like statement earrings or a red manicure!

thankful for Imanimo's wide range of party dresses that will make you party-proof, even in the third trimester. So how do they manage that? With **smart ankle-length cuts** (primarily wrap dresses that are easy to drape nicely around your belly), **perfect pleats in all the right places** and a range of **supple fabrics** in flattering colours (including always-festive metallic shades)!

THE SHOPS

BASICS / ISABELLA OLIVER

During my final months, I practically lived in Isabella Oliver's soft jumpsuits and dresses. Her long shirts with fabric ribbon are also lovely: ideal for inconspicuous cinching! **All of her designs are simple and timeless,** perfect to pimp with a not-so-basic belt or animal prints...

COMFORT / COSABELLA

I found looking for a pregnancy bra to be a pretty depressing experience. There's just sooo little choice, so I was so thrilled when I discovered Cosabella! **Made from delicate lace and available in tons of cheerful colours** (purple! coral! blue!), you couldn't tell them apart from regular lingerie, but if you look closely, you'll see that you can undo the straps to make it easier to feed your little one. A sexy mama can't do much better than that!

TRENDS / IMANIMO

If you find yourself very pregnant during wedding season (like me), you'll be extra

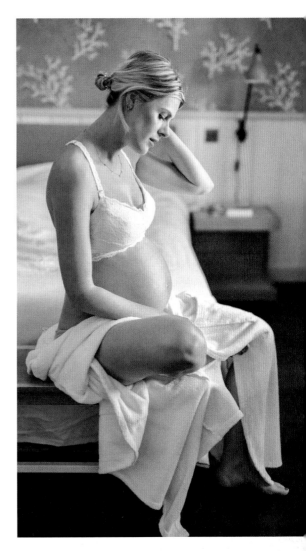

A DAY OF BABY BUMP OUTFITS AT 9 MONTHS!

No matter how hard you try to imagine how big your belly will get, you'll be huger than you could ever thought possible during the last month of your pregnancy! :) And while it can be tempting just to wear loose dresses and leggings, **it gave me so much pleasure to pick outfits that made me feel special** – always one of my favourite parts of fashion! In collaboration with Chanel (and our not-so-mini-anymore, almost-full-term baby :)) I styled a day of outfits during my last month, including a morning in the city, an outdoor lunch, and a romantic date night with my baby daddy. Memories to cherish forever!

MORNING FLOWER RUN

Contrary to what many people think, I am not all that big on shopping. I'm not particularly patient by nature, so picking things out and queuing for ages at fitting rooms and cash registers are not my thing. But picking flowers and buying ingredients for new recipes is definitely a weekly routine that I always look

forward to! **A comfy outfit with an edge** is perfect for this: a soft stretchy jumpsuit and a cosy knee-length wool cardigan (anything shorter wouldn't fall as nicely around your belly) and then **pimp out the whole thing with gold details** like a big choker chain, cross-body bag (there's nothing so annoying as a bag that's constantly slipping off your shoulder when you're out shopping!), and soft pink suede slip-on shoes (to match your bouquet, of course!).

NOON OUTDOOR LUNCH

Of course, **a lunch outfit should be comfort-**able above all, but can be a bit cooler: ripped cropped jeans (bare ankles are always more elegant) and a long cotton shirt are perfect to leave you some space for an extra piece of cake. My favourite way to bring in some extra warmth during that last month was with **an ankle-length wrap dress in a fun print, which I wore as an open summer jacket**. Add a pair of pointed loafers, a relaxed backpack and cool round sunnies, *et voilà*!

EVENING DATE WITH MY LOVE

Yup, the most difficult outfit of the day. :) The thing about date night outfits is that a dress is perfectly fine, of course, but so clichééé. I always think **it's so much more of a statement to wear trousers on a date** (we'll leave out what that says about me, lol)! But how do you get that date night vibe into your outfit? The solution is **combining contrasts!** Start with cropped jeans in a casual cut that you complement with chic over-the-top items like a white transparent blouse with puffy sleeves and bow collar, which you then tailor with a colourful knitted sleeveless cardigan. Finish it off with a fire-engine red bag and gold slippers, versus neutral sunglasses on top (you see, contrast!). And oh yeah, don't forget to get that same vibe in your manicure by interspersing your white nails with one golden glam nail per hand – 'cause mama needs her bling! ;)

BABY WARDROBE CHECKLIST:

HOW TO PUT TOGETHER
YOUR UNBORN MINI'S WARDROBE?

Confession no. 1: I have a *lot* of clothes. Confession no. 2: I am not exactly, um, tidy. Result: what was originally intended to be a nursery soon became my second (!) dressing room. *Shame on me!!* **So I know better than anyone that putting together and maintaining a thoughtful and stylish wardrobe can take quite some time and energy**, let alone when it comes to designing the wardrobe of a small person that you haven't even met! How do you handle that? And how do you avoid ending up with twenty pairs of super cute mini sneakers but no warm jackets at all? Does it actually make sense to spend (a lot of) money on things that will only be worn for a month? Take a deep breath and relax, because as you'll see, it really comes down to this: divide and conquer! :)

STEP 1: HIGH-QUALITY BASICS

If you don't know where to start when putting together your baby's wardrobe, it's a good idea to take a step back and start with the **basics that'll be worn constantly**, because besides being cute, they're very practical, too (crucial for a baby who, thanks to a few accidents here and there, changes outfits three times a day on average!). These are the pieces of which you can never have too many. How much you will exactly need depends on your love of doing laundry. I only do laundry once a week, so I've got seven to ten pieces of every basic. And if you're thinking of building an even larger family, choose more neutral colours so that future brothers or sisters can enjoy them just as much!

THE TOP 3
1. rompers
2. T-shirts, sweaters, and tops
3. shorts, skirts, and leggings

MY FAVES
THÉOPHILE & PATACHOU: best basic white/blue/pink rompers

PETIT BATEAU: iconic striped sailor sweaters and nautical prints

ROOTS & WINGS: soft sweaters and leggings in organic merino wool

HOUSE OF JAMIE: the cutest basic leggings, made with love

IMPS & ELFS: shorts with the most beautiful prints (especially in Summer!)

STEP 2: THE SPLURGES

And then it's time for **fun!** :) **It's perfectly fine to buy some ridiculously expensive or not-so-practical pieces,** simply because they're so irresistibly cute. Because how long can you dress them in a bright yellow raincoat, am I right?

THE TOP 3
1. overalls, dungarees, dresses, or rompers and swimwear with a twist
2. statement jacket (like a bright yellow raincoat or faux fur jacket!)
3. mini sneakers, knitted booties, and their first lace-up shoes

MY FAVES
MOUMOUT: tiny swim trunks, with and without frills – just too cute

BENEDITA: sailor suits! (of course that's the look we chose to introduce our mini to the world :))

TURTLEDOVE: kimono rompers and collars

DOTTY DUNGAREES: as many nostalgic overalls and pinafores as you can handle

TOCOTO VINTAGE: tiny clothes with a bohemian vibe

MINNA PARIKKA: sneakers with rabbit ears!

TOASTIE PIG: baby's first wool-lined lace-up shoes

THE LITTLE THINGS

STEP 3: ACCESSOIRES

The smallest things are often the most fun, and the same is true for your baby's wardrobe! **Because who wouldn't melt at the sight of those tiny accessories that you can enjoy to the fullest before you even know if you're having a boy or a girl?** Moreover, you're also much less limited by sizes here, because these items are so much more flexible than an average garment...

THE TOP 3

1. socks and gloves
2. hats
3. swaddles and bibs

MY FAVES

HUTTELIHUT: handmade wool pompom hats, in mini and maxi versions!

MY LITTLE COZMO: tiny cotton hats in earth tones

FRANCIS & HENRY: wonderfully soft swaddles in subtle prints

LIEWOOD: absorbent bibs in different sizes, with or without ears

THE 3 ULTIMATE DOS & DON'TS

DO: NATURAL MATERIALS, DON'T: SYNTHETIC FABRICS

I'd definitely like to pass on my personal preference for natural materials to our mini, and certainly if you know the **downsides of synthetic fabrics**: they don't breathe, they stick to your skin, and they just feel unnatural – the last thing you want for your baby!

And don't let yourself be seduced by synthetic thermal fabrics that will help you keep baby nice and warm, at least according to the advertising; wool does that just as well, and without all those scary downsides. So for all the mini clothes you buy, check the label to know the exact composition (**yay for cotton, viscose, linen, poplin, and cashmere!**).

DO: BREEZY CUT, DON'T: TIGHT FITS

One of the biggest challenges when putting together your baby's wardrobe is to estimate the right sizes! But because too small is always worse than a bit big, **you're better off going with clothing for minis that are 3 months old** (instead of 1 month). If your baby turns out to be a bit smaller, you can always bring in a few teeny tiny pieces, or you can mainly focus those first months on items that also work well if they're oversized (like a romper or sweater). Roll up the sleeves and trouser legs, and there you go!

DO: HAPPY COLOURS, DON'T: BLACK, BLACK, BLACK

Although shopping for baby clothes was a totally new experience, I knew one thing in advance: kids love colour! Whether you have a boy or girl, it's a fact that you'll always do better with a non-black wardrobe – something I can fully appreciate. Avoid neon colours and cliché prints like bears and hearts, and choose **timeless colours** (brick red, mustard yellow, sky blue, and moss green are always stylish!) and **baby-friendly geometric prints** like tiny boats or beautifully designed animals.

BABY COUNTDOWN
WHAT DO YOU TAKE
TO THE HOSPITAL?

Packing your suitcase to bring your baby into the world: it's definitely one of the most surreal mama-to-be moments! **What do you take with you to mark the start of this completely new phase in your life?** A toothbrush? Extra socks? Confetti? Champagne?
Since I was fairly (OK, very :)) nervous about my very first delivery, I did quite a bit of research, and I turned out to be super happy with my selection, which saw me surprisingly smoothly through the delivery that fateful night in May 2017...

BEAUTY

This was perhaps the most difficult bit to pack – you know, to make a distinction between what you would only use in the Hollywood version of your delivery and what would *really* come in handy. In the end, I decided to **focus mainly on helpful multitaskers:** products that are good for different things and therefore take up less space in your suitcase. **In terms of make-up, I limited myself to my favourite classics**, ideal for a touch-up during those first days after the birth; to receive your besties and family looking a little fresher.

SKIN CARE

EAU DE BEAUTÉ FACIAL MIST - CAUDALIE
Anyone who knows me knows I have a mild obsession with refreshing face mists. This is one of my all-time favourites and goes with me on every trip, to freshen up on-the-go after a long flight or a city trip. Not only refreshing, but also an instant reminder of my most beloved spots in the world: the perfect 2-in-1 calming combo! ;)

HUILE PRODIGIEUSE DRY OIL - NUXE
Another all-time favourite! This dry oil (which absorbs quickly and does not leave that typical greasy film) is the ultimate multitasker that you can apply to your face, body and hair for

deep hydration – very needed in the dry hospital atmosphere!

AVOPLEX HAND & NAIL CREAM - OPI
Again, a super-reliable anti-dry-air remedy, but specifically for hands and nails. Absorbs quickly and prevents cracking, for extra soft hands to hold your baby for the first time. :)

VILLA NOACARLINA TOOTHPASTE - LEBON
And yes, I'd even thought about my toothpaste! :) I admit that I originally bought these for the irresistible coral-and-gold packaging, but it's also a nice change from the classic mint flavour.

DRY SHAMPOO FOAM - OUAI

My search for the perfect dry shampoo literally went on for years, until this was finally launched. Thanks to the foamy texture, you don't have to worry about exposing your baby to harmful atomisers (aaah, so much worry as a new mama! :)) and it smells amazing, too!

CLEANSING WATER BABY - LA LANGERIE

That much talked-about fresh soft baby skin smell: that was one of the things I was most looking forward to when I was pregnant. :) So this 100% natural water was the only baby care product that I took along to freshen up our boy in those early days. Besides that, his skin stayed completely *au naturel!*

MAKE-UP

LIP GLOW POMADE - DIOR

Unlike many other lip balms, this nourishing pomade comes in a convenient tube! And more than anything: it's been specially developed to make the natural colour of your lips just that bit more intense – giving your complexion a boost without having to go for full-on lipstick.

SCULPTING & BRIGHTENING CONCEALER - DIOR

If you only take one make-up product with you, make it concealer! Giving birth is a marathon, to say the least, and chances are you'll get little to no sleep during those first few nights. In other words: those dark circles will have to be camouflaged, which this does perfectly.

LES BEIGES HEALTHY GLOW NATURAL EYE SHADOW PALETTE - CHANEL

Any eye shadow palette with natural shades will work wonders, especially if it makes the colour of your eyes pop!

LE VOLUME MASCARA - CHANEL

Another quick fix: a simple layer of mascara is the quickest way to brighten up your eyes (and your whole face) in an instant.

SOLEIL CONTOURING POWDER - TOM FORD

And last but not least, did you know that contouring your cheekbones, nose, and eyebrows actually has much more effect than simply applying eye shadow? It just gives so much depth to your face that it determines your whole look, in contrast with more localised make-up. So don't forget to take a quick look at a contouring tutorial before you head for the hospital!

FASHION

While the outfit you wear before and after you give birth is mainly about comfort, safety, and warmth, there's nothing to keep you from **picking clothing that just makes you feel beautiful** – in my case, natural fabrics with the quintessential flattering cut. And as my dear readers told me in advance: don't forget to bring **an extra pair of warm socks** for the delivery room, because it's always colder than you'd think.

MOMMY

SOFT UNDERWEAR AND MATERNITY BRAS - COSABELLA

This is clearly not the time to bring out your delicate light-coloured lingerie! Oversized inexpensive black cotton underpants (that you can throw away afterwards) are a much better choice. And then all that's left is to top them

WARM BOOTIES - UGG
Again, my fear of cold: fur-lined booties or slippers were packed in my suitcase weeks in advance!:)

KNIT BLANKET - MISSONI
And part III of my anti-cold offensive: you can never go wrong with a knit wool blanket.

BABY
COTTON ROMPERS, GLOVES, HATS, AND BIBS - THÉOPHILE & PATACHOU
It took an embarrassingly long time to pick out the very first outfits that our son would wear, but the most important thing is to take along a lot – all of it in natural fabrics that breathe, of course, and preferably in different sizes – because they stay clean for an average of about 0.3 seconds. :) Matching gloves are useful for securing scratching little hands, and a cotton cap and booties will keep your newborn mini nice and warm (like mama, like baby).

off with the most elegant pregnancy bra ever! (see earlier)

CASHMERE JUMPSUIT - MADELEINE THOMPSON AND SILK PYJAMAS - OLIVIA VON HALLE
Despite the fact that I finally gave birth during an exceptionally early heat wave (of course!), since I'm constantly cold anyway, I was mainly worried about being chilly in hospital. So of course a cashmere jumpsuit was ideal for the ride to and from the hospital. I was happy to wear my beloved silk pyjamas once we got there, which always look chic and feel so luxurious on the skin.

SWADDLE - FRANCIS & HENRY
I'd heard a lot of good things about swaddling your baby in a big cotton cloth (it's supposed to calm your baby because it reminds him of his time in your snug, compact belly :)) and although it felt kind of weird in the beginning to wrap him all up, even his arms, he seemed to find it comfortable and comforting.

TEDDY BEAR - THÉOPHILE & PATACHOU
Baby's first teddy bear can't be left at home, even if it's just to make those first few pictures even cuter.

PRACTICAL

No matter how hard I had tried in advance to not pack too much (always a struggle for me!)) I couldn't resist throwing in a couple of you-never-know items, **those typical things that you probably don't use every day, but that still help you feel reassured** and are a nice addition to those boring practical things you can't afford to forget.

CALMING PLAYLIST, CAMERA, BREASTFEEDING PILLOW OR BOTTLES, CAR SEAT, INSURANCE DOCUMENTS

NATURAL SCENTED CANDLES – SANUI
My 100% natural SANUI scented candle is still my favourite way to make an impersonal room feel instantly like home!

POWER FOOD AND COCONUT WATER
Like many people, I'm not a big fan of hospital food, so planning my emergency hospital stash was one of those things that I started to do ridiculously early. But guess what? I was very happy with my stash of nutritious power food bars, dark chocolate, fresh nuts and home-made quinoa cookies, not only so I could regain my strength after the delivery, but also to offer them to our little Gabriel's first visitors!

POST-BABY QUINOA COOKIES
For 30 cookies
· 2 eggs
· 200 g of regular flour
· 190 g almond butter
· 2 bananas, mashed
· 2 teaspoons of vanilla extract

- · 100 g oatmeal
- · 100 g puffed quinoa
- · 90 g dark chocolate, chopped
- · 60 g walnuts, chopped
- · 2 teaspoons of baking powder
- · 2 teaspoons of cinnamon
- · 1 tablespoon of chia seeds

optional: a few scoops of brown sugar or apple sauce

Preheat your oven to 180° C and cover a large baking sheet (or two) with parchment paper. Beat the eggs with the flaxseed flour and about 5 tablespoons of water. Mix the almond butter, bananas, and vanilla extract in a large bowl and add the egg mixture. Add the remaining ingredients and mix until you have a slightly sticky mixture. Shape balls that are about 2 tablespoons of dough and arrange them on the baking sheet, leaving enough distance in between. Bake the cookies for 15-20 minutes until the edges are golden brown.

Tip: If you want slightly sweeter cookies, add a few scoops of brown sugar or applesauce.

Beauty & wellness

Honestly? My first pregnancy was not exactly the best time in my life. It is still a bit taboo to admit it, but **I was just miserable for the first four months.** I was nauseous or vomiting day and night, I couldn't tolerate food or intense smells around me, and I was too weak to do even a simple outfit shoot... It was a major contrast to my pre-pregnancy life, and frankly a bit of a scary feeling, if you have to keep running your business and don't seem to have any control over what's happening to your body.

But, as is always the way, there was an upside, too. Those first months taught me, in a not-so-subtle way, to put **my control freak and workaholic tendencies in perspective** and to open myself up (for the first time ever!) to a new set of priorities. That, an amazing concealer, and a few other cheeky tricks helped me make it in the end, and although I know it seemed a small consolation at the time, believe me, **once you see those little toes for the first time, it'll all have been more than worth it!**

HOW TO FAKE
THE PREGNANCY GLOW

You know how people always talk about that pregnancy glow or how you're naturally radiant from the pure happiness of carrying your baby? Not so much in my case! :) After weeks of exhaustion and running back and forth from the bathroom to the couch, the eyes of our fat grey cat Bobke were the only thing that shone radiantly in our house; it was so much fun for him to finally have a night-time buddy! But hey, **if you're not naturally glowing, just fake it**. Even after those difficult months, I kept coming back to these three glowing beauty rescuers. Because baby or no baby: don't you just always want to be radiant?!

COPPER-GOLDEN EYE STYLO FOR BRIGHTER EYES - CHANEL STYLO EYESHADOWS BEIGE DORÉ

It's Kim K's most famous beauty trick, so it must be a winner: a brassy 'undereye', or shimmery copper line under your eyes! It makes your eyes instantly look bigger, making your whole face look more awake, especially if you're going for an ombre effect, with a golden yellow hue in the corner of your eye that subtly transitions into a darker copper and/or brown.

BLUSH HIGHLIGHTER FOR A HEALTHY GLOW - BOBBI BROWN SUNSET GLOW HIGHLIGHTER

The highlighter: everyone's No. 1 go-to to add a bit more depth to your face and create a healthy glow! I took quite a long time to find the perfect shade for my skin, and it turned out that it actually tops almost all my friends' favourites list. The rosy undertone is perfect for a healthy blush, while the golden glitter adds a warm finish. In other words: highlighter perfection!

SHIMMERING DRY OIL FOR RADIANT HAIR - ESTÉE LAUDER BRONZE GODDESS SHIMMERING OIL

Another miracle worker is this shimmering dry oil! You can use it both on your hair and body, and it really is the easiest way to make your hair shine. I don't like lightweight sprays because at least half of every spritz always ends up anywhere but in your hair, so an oil is also ideal in that sense. Oh, and it smells delicious too!

P.S. And to counter those two other well-known pregnancy ailments – stretch marks and hair loss – I used the 100% natural **Anti-Stretch Marks Serum from the French brand Eve & Rose** (made by a mama who couldn't find a completely safe good-smelling serum during her pregnancy, so she made one herself!) and the **Dry Scalp & Hair Treatment shampoo from Mediceuticals,** specially developed to prevent female hair loss, with mint extract to give you a wonderful tingling sensation when you wash your hair!

BABY BUMP VS. HEAT WAVE:
YOU WILL SURVIVE

When I found out I was pregnant in October, I was jumping for joy immediately: yay, it'll be a spring baby!! It's not just a fun time to celebrate your birthday (for baby) but it also means you'll escape being extremely pregnant during the hottest part of the year (for mama). Fast forward to 9 months later and yes, **there I was, puffing away with my round belly during an exceptional (of course) heat wave in May!** It's not hard to imagine how these cool tricks helped keep me sane…

COOL DOWN BEAUTY

GRANADO REFRESCANTE PINK CREAM

The Brazilians know how to make hot days more bearable, so every time I visit my in-laws I come home with a few tubes of this cooling cream! **The gel-like texture spreads easily and absorbs quickly into your skin,** unlike most other creams that only make you feel warmer. Don't forget to apply some just before you go to sleep, to cool down at night.

COOL DOWN DESIGN

MUJI MINI FAN

When I bought my powder pink mini fan in the Japanese store MUJI in Paris, I thought: will this be one of those things you buy because it's cute and never use? But no! On the hottest days, it's brought a breeze to our un-air-conditioned house for years (because who has air conditioning in Belgium?). **Because it's so small and has a USB port you can plug it in anywhere,** even on the go. And on those days you don't need it, it's also a beautiful addition in your décor!

COOL-DOWN DRINKS

DIY SUMMERY MOCKTAIL

Okay, okay, it might be a bit of a poor alternative to the real deal, but cocktails without alcohol can really be delicious! They're around **100 times more refreshing** than their alcoholic counterparts, and… **you'll never ever get a hangover.** Doesn't sound so bad, does it?

PINEAPPLE-ELDERFLOWER MOCKTAIL

· 1 tablespoon of elderflower syrup
· 100 ml fresh pineapple juice
  (plus a few chunks of pineapple)
· 150 ml ice water
· 1 tablespoon of fresh lime juice
· a handful of fresh mint leaves

Add all the ingredients, plus a little ice cream, to a cocktail shaker or lockable can and shake for half a minute. Pour, add some fresh mint leaves, and a slice of lime and/or pineapple.

LET'S TALK FOOD!

As a true foodie, this was something I looked forward to from the beginning of my pregnancy: the cravings! **Which treats would suddenly become 100% irresistible, and how many minor food dramas awaited us** – including night-time fridge raids and desperate midnight quests for ice cream, now, immediately, right this moment?! And guess what happened during those first months... nothing at all! My sense of smell was over-developed and my stomach was so sensitive that I could barely think of food, let alone develop cravings.
But old habits die hard, and it was the **whole-grain waffles from my dad** that got me through that phase! And yes, once my appetite for food came back (around the 4th month) there were two unexpected things that I suddenly *had* to have every day: **citrus fruit in every possible form** (bring on the grapefruit!) and **simple sugars** (like sodas). Never before had I been a big soft drink fan, but during my pregnancy it suddenly seemed like the best drink in the world. :) I finally came up with a version that was so healthy I could go through litres of it without guilt, lol. And because I was often too tired to cook, Marcio, whose main specialty is easy pasta recipes, often took over. And in the number 1 spot, you guessed it, **pasta with lemon**.
Hoping against hope that our baby would come out nice and chunky,
packing cute little rolls in reserve!

FIRST TRIMESTER POWER FOOD

DADDY DEAR'S WHOLE WHEAT WAFFLES
· 300 g white flour
· 200 g spelt or whole wheat flour
· 300 g vanilla sugar
· 1 teaspoon of dry yeast
· 2 teaspoons of vanilla pudding powder
· 6 eggs
· 400 g butter, olive oil or coconut oil
· pinch of salt

Put the flour, sugar, dry yeast and vanilla
pudding powder in a blender. Add the eggs
and melted butter or oil, and the pinch of
salt. Run the blender for a few minutes at low
speed until you achieve a smooth batter. Allow
to rest for about an hour at room temperature
and... bake away!

MY TOP-3 CRAVINGS

STRAWBERRY-COCONUT SODA
· 5 fresh strawberries
· 125 ml ice-cold carbonated water
· 250 ml ice-cold unsweetened coconut water
· 1 tablespoon of fresh lemon juice
optional: 1 teaspoon of agave syrup or 100 ml
ginger juice

Mix the strawberries and the carbonated water
in a blender and strain it (if necessary) to remove the seeds. Add the other ingredients and
shake. Serve ice cold!
Tip: For a sweeter or spicier version, you can
add a little agave syrup or ginger juice.

SPRING CITRUS SALAD
For 3-4 people
· 150 g bulghur, cooked and cooled
· 3 blood oranges, thinly sliced
· 3 red beets, toasted and thinly sliced
· 1 small fennel bulb, thinly sliced
· 1-2 teaspoons of olive or walnut oil
· a handful of pomegranate seeds
· 130 g manouri cheese
· ½ teaspoon of sea salt
· a dash of pepper
· a handful of fresh coriander

Mix the bulghur, blood oranges, beets and fennel together with the oil and spices in a large
bowl. Toss carefully until everything is nicely
distributed. Add the pomegranate seeds and

manouri, and season with a little pepper and fresh coriander. Let the mixture sit at room temperature for a little bit so that the flavours of the ingredients can mingle. Enjoy!

PASTA AL LIMONE
For 3-4 people
· 300 g linguine
· 2-3 teaspoons of olive oil
· 50 ml cream
· 2 tablespoons of organic lemon peel, grated
· grated Parmesan, to taste
· 3 tablespoons of fresh lemon juice
· a handful of fresh basil
· salt and pepper, to taste

Add the pasta to boiling water with a pinch of salt or broth and cook until al dente according to the instructions on the package. Drain (keep the water!) and add a splash of olive oil to prevent the pasta from sticking together. Put 50 ml of the cooking liquid back in your cooking pot, add the cream, olive oil and lemon zest, and cook for a few minutes. Remove the pot from the heat and add pasta, cheese, lemon juice and basil. If necessary, add a little more water if the mixture is too thick. Season with pepper and salt.

WORK, WORK, WORK:
3 TIPS TO *TRULY*
EMBRACE THE CALM

When Marcio and I found out I was pregnant, we were completely shocked: **how could we possibly be pregnant during one of the busiest times of our lives??** We were so happy, and right away I secretly hoped it would be a sign for my entire pregnancy: easy peasy, feeling a child grow in your belly while you live your life just like before, without too many adjustments ... A few weeks later: reality check! For the first time in my life the accumulated over-fatigue of the Fashion Weeks struck hard, and that was a big surprise for my workaholic self! It was clear: **if I wanted to get myself and our baby through this pregnancy happy and healthy, I had to take it a little easier**. And it won't surprise you that these five super-simple adjustments had such a big impact that I still happily use them today, post-baby. Because a relaxed mother is a relaxed baby – most of the time, at least. ;)

TAKE A MOMENT OUT OF YOUR DAY TO DO SOMETHING QUIET FOR YOURSELF
It may sound super-logical now, but it took a while before I realised that my busy brain is a direct result of my general (over)sensitivity. My senses are always, always, always sharp, and the smells, sounds, tastes, things I feel and see come at me 100%, without filters or nuances. That can be wonderful – because it allows you to experience positive experiences to the fullest – but it's also very exhausting! So **taking at least one moment every day to consciously close your mind to all those impulses** is an amazing way to create calm: just browsing through my favourite magazine with Bobke in my lap, throwing open the windows and taking a nap or meditating... **Even if it only takes 20 minutes, it impacts my entire day.** So it's definitely worth the effort!

PLAN AN (IMAGINARY) GETAWAY

Anyone who knows me knows how much I love travelling – discovering new places, immersing myself in a completely different culture, tasting delicious dishes and finding little handmade treasures at local markets... it's paradise! So if I feel stressed, planning a (real or imaginary) future getaway is the perfect way to relax. **When I'm looking at my favourite destinations it feels like I'm already there**, but without the annoying jetlag! And it was ideal for helping me get used to the idea of travelling with our mini – a major change, but sooo lovely.

REDECORATE!

This may sound a little strange at first, but changing something about your décor can really have a big impact on your mood and your stress levels. That's where we get the idea of spring cleaning – **you clean up your house and your state of mind at the same time**, and since it's something I'm always putting off, it gives me so much satisfaction when I do get to it (I do try not to limit it to spring, though, and **do a deep clean at the start of every season** instead). Especially if you travel a lot, being able to truly relax in your home is extra important, right?

S.O.S. PARENTHOOD

HOW DO YOU PREPARE
FOR BECOMING PARENTS?

Preparing to become a mama or papa: totally impossible? Since nothing or no
one in the world can predict how you will feel your post-delivery and – more
importantly – how your baby will be as a person, there seems to be some truth in
it. And although I'm certainly not the person who's memorised 101 maternity and
baby books, there are **a few things that reassured me a bit as a future mama**, and in
any case made me feel like I had covered the basics of what was coming...

LISTEN TO YOUR PARENTS AND YOUR BESTIES

**My family has always been super impor-
tant to me, doubly so during my pregnancy!**
Telling my parents that their first grandchild
was on the way was one of the most beautiful
moments of my life. And both my mama's advice and my papa's home-made waffles (which
I talked about before) made my pregnancy
so much more enjoyable. And I also relied so
much on my besties, who didn't shy away from
any of my hugely embarrassing questions,
lol. Is going to the bathroom every 2 seconds
normal during your third trimester? (yup) Will
I be able to travel with a newborn baby? (also
yup) So instead of ploughing through stacks
of baby books: **get real advice from people
who love you!**

IDENTIFY YOUR ANXIETIES (AND TALK ABOUT THEM!)

I'm certainly not a super anxious person by
nature, but **being pregnant for the first time
confronted me with a whole array of new
fears**. What if the baby just cries non-stop the
first two years of his life? What if he doesn't
like me at all? How can we fit him into our

busy life without stressing him (and ourselves)
out too much? The list seemed endless, and
during those first few months, which I was
forced to spend mostly in the office, it really drove me crazy! And the hardest thing:
Talking about it felt I was a bad mother.
When I finally spoke to a friend about it, she
immediately reassured me: **it's just part of
your natural maternal instinct to worry!** So if
you feel anxious during your pregnancy, don't
bottle it up. Talk about it, even if it feels a bit
weird. You'll feel so much better afterwards!

TACKLE YOUR BABY TO-DO LIST BY FOLLOWING THE TOP-3 METHOD

You may have already noticed: I am a big fan
of divide-and-conquer! If you've got a lot of
work and a chaotic brain, it's the only thing
that really works, in my opinion. The concept
is very simple: **every three days, make a top-3
list of your priority tasks and cross one off
your list every day.** Turns out, it's not so much
the content of your to-do list that you get
stuck on, it's the length. So if you limit yourself to focusing on one thing a day, it's easier
to push through!

SEE YOUR BABY AS A FUN PERSON

In between all those new (often irrational) anxieties and the prospect of a lot of sleepless nights, you might almost forget that your baby is probably going to be a really lovely person! It's okay to prepare for the worst-case scenarios in your life, but sometimes it's healthier to keep a cool head and realise that the chances of a baby crying non-stop for two years is smaller than them being an amazing kid. **Basically, your baby will be an amazing mix of you and the love of your life.** Now that doesn't sound so scary, does it?

KEEP YOUR NO.1 GOAL AS A PARENT IN MIND

It's easy to lose yourself in all of the parental duties that await you. That's one of the biggest pitfalls for every mama-to-be, especially if you're a perfectionist like me. **Instead, try to focus on that one main goal that you want to achieve more than anything as a parent!** For us, it was so simple: to have a happy and open-minded child who is uninhibited by anxieties as much as possible. Once you have that goal in your mind, it'll be a lot easier to add tasks that will hopefully help you reach it, like letting your baby try out as many new experiences, places, and people as possible, in a way that makes him feel safe and confident. And remember: it's supposed to be tons of fun!

FROM NORTH TO BLUE IVY:
HOW DO YOU PICK THE PERFECT NAME?

You know that feeling? When a friend tells a random story about someone named Alexander
or Caroline, and you immediately think of a person with the same name that you'd rather
not be reminded of? :) Names are anything but objective. Add in your personal taste and all
the practical considerations, and it's very clear: **picking a baby name isn't as easy it looks**.
Fortunately, there are a few super-handy tricks that can really help as you make one of the most
important decisions of your life (no pressure) ... And if you really can't figure something out, just
wait until he or she arrives and make a spontaneous choice – very Hollywood!

IMAGINE WHAT YOUR BABY WILL BE LIKE

Of course, a name is much more than a bunch
of letters, it's something that can affect your
whole identity. From powerful to sweet to
traditional, a name says a lot about baby and
parents alike. And that's exactly why it is so
difficult to choose a name for your unborn
baby. How do you pick a name if you don't
know anything about his or her personality?
What helped us so much was **knowing the
sex of our baby in advance** and studying the
ultrasound photos (too :)) carefully. It not
only made me very curious and impatient to
meet our mini as quickly as possible, but also
allowed us to form **a vague idea of what he'd
look like** (delicate head, strong jaw line, big
hands!), which in turn was incredibly helpful
in choosing his name.

of our top 10 favourite names, from which we eventually culled to **a top 3 of our joint favourites.** Super convenient and (almost) completely argument-free! :)

THE CHOICE: THREE FINAL DECISIONS

And then it's time to choose! This is undoubtedly the most difficult phase. Now you have three names that you really like, but **how do you choose the one**? Fortunately, there are three things that really help: start by **combining every name with your baby's surname to see what works best**. Some of the first names are beautiful on their own, but they don't add up when you combine them with the baby's last name.

It can also help to imagine **your baby at every stage of his life**. When choosing a baby name, it's so tempting to go ultra cute: you're imagining the cutest baby in the world, so that includes a cute name, right? But remember that your baby will eventually become an adult, too, and then it might not be so fun to go through life named Little Rolfie. :) Take a moment to imagine your mini as a maxi before you make the final choice!

And now to the final decider: **is the name practical?** Simply merging your top 3 into one long, gigantic name may seem like the solution to your analysis paralysis, but chances are your baby won't be as happy. No matter how boring it sounds, don't forget to take the practical side into account, too.

RESEARCH, RESEARCH, RESEARCH

Okay, researching baby names might be a bit overwhelming. There are soooo many lists and options! But once I had a bit of an impression of what our little guy would be like, I had a lot of fun finding inspiration on classic baby name lists. Decide in advance whether you'd prefer a **popular or unusual name**, and whether you'd rather have a **more international name**. For example, do you want to use a certain nationality as a guideline, like we did with Brazilian to tie in Marcio's home country, or is it important for you that the name can be pronounced easily in different countries? That'll make your search a lot easier! And from there it is just a matter of research, research and more research.

TOP 10 TO TOP 3

You probably already know this, but I like to make lists. And they came in handy when choosing our baby's name! To avoid a Ross & Rachel situation, where both partners throw down endless vetoes to each other's suggestions, **my boyfriend and I each made a list**

Design

By now it's clear that when it comes to preparing for the arrival of your baby, there's a lot to do, from making sure your fashion, beauty & food game is on point and coming up with a perfect name, to putting together your baby's wardrobe and preparing yourself emotionally and physically for the delivery. It can be pretty overwhelming. There will be days that you'll be totally done with all those practical to-do lists, but it's a safe bet that this part will make up for a lot of the hassle: it's time to design! Setting up the baby nursery and picking out birth announcements were things I was looking forward to from the very beginning, and since I just had no energy during the first few months, it was twice as fun when I finally got around to it. They are two of the most love-filled creative projects I've ever worked on, and the result was exactly as I'd imagined it: max satisfaction!

BABY NURSERY:
A COZY SPOT FOR OUR LITTLE BOY

Yesss, designing the baby nursery – let's do this!! Those were my literal words during month 4, followed by a mildly worried look from my boyfriend. Wasn't I forgetting one important detail? Mmm, yes... Over time, the room that was originally destined for a mini when we bought our house had turned into my second dressing room, home to an embarrassingly huge assortment of sassy accessories that I couldn't get rid of. So if we were honest, step 1 was: **clear out closet 2, clean up and repaint the room, and then... the fun part!**

STEP 1. GET INSPIRED

There's nothing I'd rather do on a rainy afternoon than settle into a chair with our fluffy cat Bobke and a cup of hot chocolate and browse through a bunch of magazines. That's how my love of fashion started, and I always get so much inspiration from it! **It's really important to get an idea of what you want beforehand, especially for a design project you're not familiar with** (like designing your first nursery). Mood boards where you collect examples of your favourite styles are perfect for that! After a few on- and offline inspiration sessions, I finally settled on these four favourites!

PRACTICAL

It probably had something to do with the fact that the room was such a mess in the initial phase, but in any case, the idea of a practical nursery really appealed to me from the beginning. Plus, the shape of the room was quite a challenge (see p. 62), so **smart space-saving tricks** (super simple things like a copper rod under a shelf to hang little jackets) seemed like a winning plan to me!

ALL NATURAL

Nature has always had a calming effect on me, so it was pretty much my hope that natural pieces in the baby nursery would have the same effect on our mini. **Warm materials** like wood and organic cotton, **little plants or dried flowers**, and a **natural colour palette** with green and brick red; can't you just picture a happy little baby there?

CLEAN

I am a fan of a bright interiors anyway, with lots of fresh whites and not too much stuff. **It just relaxes me to have only the essentials in a room** – beautiful versions of them, of course. And although it definitely won't stay white for long with those little wandering hands, it seemed like a good starting point! :)

DREAMY

To keep the clean vibe from feeling chilly, I went all in with dreamy details that would **make the room sweet and cosy**. A lovely dangling mobile, cheerful pillows, or pennants and twinkle lights along the bed: who could object to that!

STEP 2. LET'S BE PRACTICAL

After dreaming away at my mood boards, we hit the reality check: you can hardly imagine a more impractical space than the room we wanted to turn into a baby nursery. :) It's a fairly small room with a whimsical shape, characteristic of an authentic town house, right under the roof with original supporting beams on both sides. Add to that the fact that a nursery should serve all kinds of functions (dressing, sleeping, and changing) and it was definitely a question of **measuring, planning, and drawing** before we went shopping at the baby store! Every room is different, of course, but try to set up your room to **expose your baby to a lot of natural light** (by putting the crib next to the window, for instance) and get as many **2-in-1 pieces** as you can, like a dresser that includes a changing pad. Babies always need more stuff than you expect, so **the more storage space, the better!**

it didn't seem very practical for the future. Who knows if there will be a brother or sister later who won't fit mini no. 1's colour scheme at all?! Add to that my innate love for that bright vibe and it was clear that **white would be the main colour of the room**. We found all of our big furniture – wardrobe, dresser, floor lamp, bed, and storage baskets – at Théophile & Patachou. They have a wonderful collection if you're looking for furniture with a timeless look (with classic details like carved legs and handles) that are fresh and contemporary at the same time.

STEP 3. CHOOSE A THEME AND GENERAL COLOUR SCHEME

One thing was clear from the very beginning: a typical blue or pink colour scheme was not an option for us. Apart from being a bit cliché,

STEP 4. ADD FUN!

And then... the finishing touches! A nursery should also be fun, of course, so what's true of your outfits is true of your nursery: it's the

accessories that really make it. Apart from
'normal' things like pillows and teddy bears,
**I especially enjoyed adding some special
pieces**: framed baby animals above the dresser,
a gold mini giraffe and matching vase with
purple flowers, wooden toys and a Sophie-la-
Girafe toy (we really couldn't resist!), a dreamy
mobile, panda laundry basket, pennants on the
bed, and – my personal favourite – a big sleepy
octopus on top of the wardrobe.

MY FAVES

THÉOPHILE & PATACHOU: for timeless tiny
furniture, storage baskets, and the softest
teddy bears

ANIMAL PRINT SHOP: the sweetest (baby)
animal prints!

BIG STUFFED: the only shop that makes really
beautiful and original giant stuffed animals :)

LIEWOOD: cloud-shaped cushions, panda laundry baskets or toy storage, cheerful pennants,
and mobiles

SARAH & BENDRIX: the loveliest wooden toys,
so nostalgic, and beautiful in the nursery too

AND HERE HE IS!
INTRODUCING YOUR BABY TO THE WORLD

One of the things that surprised me most as an expecting mama: **damn, it's hard to make important baby announcements in a non-clichéd way!** Before you know it, you're standing in the middle of a wheat field holding a bunch of blue confetti and wondering what on earth you're doing. :) In the end, we decided it would be more fun to keep it sweet and simple for both the pregnancy announcement and the announcement of the baby's gender – with tiny shoes and blue balloons and a designer dress (of course :)) in the sun. But when we were coming up with something sweet to serve our first visitors after the birth, and **designing our birth announcements, we wanted something special**, a personal, timeless, unique concept that completely captured the significance of the birth of our first child. It was a delicate project, but in the end these simple steps helped us achieve our dream result – including sweets and a dash of fashion, of course!

STEP 1. CHOOSE A COLOUR PALETTE

Just like the nursery, the process of designing the sweet treats and birth announcements started by deciding on our favourite colour palette. It'll come as no surprise that we didn't pick pink or blue but... white! **Since you can go all sorts of directions with this colour, it was easy to add a bit of luxury:** embossed letters in gold foil and a bit of gold wire – sometimes it can really be that simple!

STEP 2. SIMPLE IS BETTER

The biggest trap in making birth announcements (or any announcements for important life events) is that you might be tempted to translate your enthusiasm into over-the-top design, including glitter, gigantic letters and neon colours. Ironically, this often has the opposite effect, since it distracts from the special occasion. And it's generally not all that

sold. A closer look at the sweets and the temporary tattoos revealed the text 'Made With Love' or 'Gabriel Bastos' – **the perfect way to turn all the treats into a coherent whole**, so it really became a miniature Gabriel collection. Perfect for a fashion baby, lol. :)

STEP 4. CANDY & THINGS

And yes, **Gabriel's Brazilian roots were also reflected in the sweet treats handed out after his birth**, and in my very favourite way, too: chocolate! It seemed like a super-fun idea to have **various options** for the gifts, since not everyone enjoys the same things: a white lollipop with a tiny card, a little mousseline bag containing tiny heart-shaped candies, a cardboard box with the traditional white sugar beans (and one golden one!), or a temporary tattoo. And if someone had a hard time picking a single gift, they could take one of each!

MY FAVE

SOFIE DEBOUTTE: celebrating the birth of a child with gorgeous, timeless sweet treats and announcements with a personal detail

stylish, either. **Ideally, you'll want to opt for high-quality paper, a small font and classic shapes.**

STEP 3. ADD A PERSONAL DETAIL

Once you have a stylish foundation, it's time to really personalise your design. It was important for us – like it was when we were choosing his name – that **Gabriel's Brazilian roots were subtly reflected** in the sweet treats and cards we designed for his birth. Once we came up with the concept of a circle of stars, referencing the Brazilian flag, we were immediately

Travel

TRAVELING DURING PREGNANCY:
HERE'S WHAT YOU NEED TO KNOW

Travelling is one of my great passions, and has always been an important part of my life! So I'm sure you won't be surprised that I was delighted when I had enough energy to get back out on the road again after four months of feeling terrible. Until I bought our plane tickets and ticking the box 'pregnant' opened up a whole bunch of fine print. Yikes! :) After a bit of research, it was clear: **travelling with a baby bump isn't a problem at all, as long as you take a couple minor details into account**. So if you simply can't wait to turn your unborn child into a world citizen, go for it! No time like the present.

FLYING WITH THE BUMP: IS IT SAFE?
In principle, you're allowed to board a plane until about 36 weeks, but some airlines require a doctor's certificate stating you're safe to fly after your seventh month. If you're pregnant with twins or triplets, that cut-off point is often several weeks earlier! **To be absolutely sure, I always checked with the doctor first to make sure it was still safe for me to fly before every trip I took abroad**, regardless of the airline's rules. Better to play it safe than to have that baby in mid-flight, right? :)

COMFY IN THE AIR
The biggest challenge of flying with a tiny person in your belly: comfort. We all know that those plane seats can be kind of a tight fit even without a baby, so it's not hard to imagine that it's even less comfortable when you're pregnant. Fortunately, there are a few tricks that can make any flight a lot more pleasant...

STRATEGIC SEATING
Book a seat in the middle of the plane near the wings to minimise the effects of air turbulence, or try to get a bulkhead seat (near the toilets, with more leg room). In any case, choose an **aisle seat**, so you don't have to make the person beside you get up when you have to go to the bathroom every two seconds – ridiculously frequent trips to the toilet are normal during pregnancy. :)

LAYERS, LAYERS, LAYERS & NO SHOES
For the same reason, it's also a good idea to choose an outfit that's **easy to take off and put on again** (one-piece jumpsuit: nope, cashmere tracksuit and T-shirt: yes!). And as always, think **layers**. During my pregnancy, I was much, much more susceptible to cold, and since planes are always chilly, a nice warm woolly cardigan and an extra lap blanket are must-haves.
You'll definitely want to take along a **pair of (cute) warm socks** in your carry-on bag, since it's best to take off your shoes for most of the flight to avoid puffy feet and ankles! If you could use a bit of extra support, it's a good tip

to wear **support stockings or leggings** under your outfit to avoid swollen legs or lower back pain (Blanqi has the best; see above).

WALK IT OFF

You're more prone to developing blood clots during pregnancy, so it's extra important to keep your blood flowing during the flight! Try to **walk around in the aisles briefly once an hour** and **get your muscles moving**. Just stretching your legs is enough; you don't have to go through a full aerobic workout!

SAFETY FIRST

Even if you're just a couple months pregnant (and your baby bump isn't all that big yet), it's best to **fasten your safety belt around your hips** instead of over your bump. That avoids putting pressure on your uterus. It's not dangerous to your baby if you put the seatbelt over your belly, but it's so much more comfortable not to!

FOOD & DRINKS

Another charming side effect of being pregnant is that your digestive system is a lot more sensitive than usual. **Before and during the flight, avoid eating foods that make you feel bloated** (like beans or cabbage), since the effect will be intensified during air travel. And to avoid making even more trips to the bathroom, it's better to **avoid coffee or tea**, since both beverages can act as a diuretic. Water is a perfect way to stay well hydrated, though!

FASHION WEEK +1:
HOW TO DO IT WITH A BABY BUMP!

Attending one of the most hectic fashion events during the third trimester of your pregnancy:
it may not sound like the most brilliant plan, but hey, if you really love fashion
all *that* much… :) And besides, after months of resting at home, I was actually **looking forward
to being out & about in Paris, where it all started**: my career, but also our baby adventure!
So yes, if you have a glamorous event in the last few months of your pregnancy that you
absolutely don't want to miss, you can go ahead and enjoy it.
Do keep these 5 tips in mind:

PLAN IT

Planning ahead a bit is always a good idea when you're doing something for the first time, and that's twice as important when you're carrying along a pregnant belly – especially a huge one! Try to work out as many details as possible for your day or week, and come up with **a kind of scenario** for the most important plans of the day: what and where you'll eat, how you'll get around, what you're going to wear, etc. By listing the fixed elements and creating some peace of mind for yourself, it'll be much easier for you to deal with unexpected factors that pop up, especially if your mind is as crazy-busy as mine is.

OUT-OF-THE-BOX STYLING

Full disclosure: the white Dior mini-dress that I wore to their exclusive Haute Couture show with my 5-month baby bump was strategically concealed with a cropped jacket. :) In case you were wondering: catwalk sizes aren't exactly ideal for later in your pregnancy, so **covering zippers that won't close any more, adopting items from the men's collective, and getting extra creative with layers and accessories** is the way to go! A new body shape requires new styling tricks – and then it's just a matter of hoping everything stays neatly where it's supposed to...

DON'T GO TOO FAR

This one was mainly about how difficult the first couple of months were for me, but despite my great love of travel and distant destinations, I found it reassuring during my third trimester to **focus on events close to home**. Braving a crowd of street-style photographers is one thing after a short train trip, but it's a whole different kettle of fish after landing in NYC with horrible jetlag.

BACK TO BASICS

Before I got pregnant, it was easy for me to ignore basic needs like food or sleep for a while without too much impact (workaholic, yes I was!), but that obviously wasn't a good plan with our baby in my belly. Don't forget to incorporate those basic needs into your day's schedule as much as possible, **get enough sleep and always bring along a couple of super-nutritious snacks** (like nuts or power-bars) in your clutch. Also! While you're pregnant, there's a decent chance that you'll be **much more sensitive to heat or cold,** so after my experience at the Dior Haute

Couture show – where I stood there shivering in a summery mini-dress with bare legs – I arranged a couple of nice warm jackets for my next few outfits.

TRUST YOUR INSTINCTS

During my pregnancy, I noticed that almost all of my body was changing. That was one of the most surprising things. A growing belly is expected, of course, but who would have thought that I'd be dealing with constant nauseas, incredibly puffy ankles, and an urgent trip to the bathroom every 5 minutes?? Yup, it's not the most elegant time of your life, but it's so important to trust your body and try to see all those changes as something beautiful. You're making a tiny person in there; no wonder it has such an immense impact! **Try to see every change as a specific way that your body is preparing for your new baby's arrival**: I'll bet that you'll notice your lower back pain much less when you imagine how your mini is nestling safe and warm in your belly! There's a reason it's a cliché: your body really does know what it's doing. You got this!

5 TIPS FOR HAVING
THE BABYMOON
OF YOUR DREAMS

Not all traditional 'before baby' events are my thing. I deliberately avoided throwing a baby shower, since the concept really didn't appeal to me :) – but **taking a trip with my baby daddy to enjoy one last special moment with just the two of us**? Don't have to ask me twice! So when I was 8 months pregnant, we packed our bags for a five-day trip to the delightful Les Sources de Caudalie, a luxurious resort surrounding by the vineyards of Bordeaux: ideal for spending some quality time for two. It was so great for both of us to get away from all the practical baby preparations for a bit. If you're totally pro babymoon yourself, these are the things you really have to arrange!

DECADENT BRUNCHES, EVERY. SINGLE. DAY

Anyone who knows me is well aware of my obsession with breakfast. And my favourite version is obviously a wonderful weekend brunch: sleeping in late, wrapping your softest bathrobe around you, and taking the time to make all your favourite snacks – from my 'morning elixir' (hot ginger lemon tea with turmeric and mint) to avocado toast, fresh fruit and coconut water. Since **this yummy ritual will be supplanted** by short nights, early mornings and bottle feedings anyway, **at least for the first few months-with-baby**, starting the day with a decadent brunch was one of my must-haves on this trip. I mainly wanted savoury dishes every morning, which the chef at our getaway prepared with tender loving care: tiny quinoa quiches with fresh herbs, fish, wonderfully aromatic bread, fried eggs… all decorated with the loveliest spring blossoms! So beautiful and soooo delicious!!

TREAT YOURSELF BIG-TIME

As you can tell, our babymoon was all about doing the things we enjoy so much, the things that we'd need to (temporarily) put on hold once our baby arrived. And spending a whole day swanning from massage to jacuzzi to face mask to the next massage was definitely part of that process! :) So that's exactly what we did, over and over – because **enjoying luxurious pampering without a care in the world** is exactly what you need as mamas and papas to be.

FOCUS ON YOU AS A COUPLE (AND TAKE THOSE CHEESY PHOTOS)

And then there's the narrative about becoming a mama and papa: don't let that be the main theme of your babymoon – no matter how silly that might sound! The next few months will be 100% about your baby, so why not take a couple moments for yourself now, while you still have time? **Doing fun things that you've never done together before** is always a perfect way to fall in love all over again. We took a

tour of the expansive vineyards – so romantic! And sure, go ahead and **take those cheesy couple photos**! Believe me, you'll be glad you did. :)

STYLE IT

Another thing that I missed during the last few months of my pregnancy (and would probably still miss for a while after our baby arrived): styling my outfits with meticulous care! If you love fashion as much as I do, any serious restrictions on the outfits you can wear are really irritating, so **I lavished extra attention on the outfits I took along on our babymoon**: a casual look with a blouse, denim, fluffy sandals and a sun hat for exploring the area, a simple pool-side look with an off-the-shoulders dress, a headband and big earrings, or a traditional caftan-and-oversized-sunglasses combo. It instantly made me feel like I was on holiday!

DAYDREAM ABOUT THE FUTURE TOGETHER

Even though we spent the whole trip focusing mainly on us as a couple, as I said above, it was also really fun now and then to **spend time daydreaming about the near future together**: what would he look like (fluffy Brazilian curls, please!), would he be just as wiggly as he was in my belly, what personality traits of ours would he inherit...? Could anything be more fun than daydreaming with the love of your life about the tiny person you two made together? I don't think so. :)

PART TWO

HE'S
HERE!

Antwerp, May 30th, 2017.
Went to bed extra early so I could make the most of my short
nights. It's really not all that easy to sleep with a gigantic belly
full of wide-awake wiggly Brazilian baby! :) I woke up in the
middle of the night in a sopping-wet nightgown: what's going
on now? I got up to put on a new nightdress and went back
to bed, because when your water breaks, that's got to be more
than this, right? A bit later, the same thing happened again.
I went ahead and woke Marcio up (yup, he sleeps through
everything :)) and told him: **I think it's time**.

And yes, fast-forward to the morning, and there he was: **our Gabriel Bastos, 3.460 kilos and 54 cm**. He arrived as the neatest, tidiest baby ever, just perfect with his long legs and big feet, tiny little nose and contemplative gaze, looking slightly surprised at his own birth. :)

My friends and my mama had told me over and over that it would happen, but nothing could have prepared me for that feeling of holding our child in my arms for the first time: so many emotions in that one moment! What on earth is this??

AND THERE HE IS:
OUR LITTLE
GABRIEL BASTOS!

Preparing for becoming a mama is one thing, but being a mama is a whole different thing: How do you fit your mini into your new morning and evening rituals? How do you deal with sleepless nights, and what are the best 'baby dates' for spending some fun quality time with your little monkey? What are the cutest outfits for your post-baby body? What if you really can't keep yourself from dressing identical to your mini sometimes? What gifts would you really prefer to get as a new mama? Oh yes, and what about travelling with a baby; is that a guaranteed disaster on the plane? I've written about all that and more here, authentically and without sugar-coating it. While cloud nine certainly isn't a total myth, sometimes your cloud is in dire need of a silver lining – and then it's extra fun to have a couple of tricks up your sleeve! :)

Fashion

Would you rather have a boy or a girl? That's something that everyone wonders (isn't it? :)) and in my case, I have to confess that I originally felt a slight preference for having a girl. There wasn't really a super-rational reason for it; it just intuitively seemed easier to build a bond with a girl, and yes, I already had a Hollywood-style scene with our shared dressing room in my head, lol.

But that totally changed once I saw the first ultrasound of our little boy (what a cliché, I know): whether it was a boy, a girl, or something in between, this was our tiny baby, and those handbags and high heels could wait. And guess what: as the months passed, I had more and more fun putting together our mini's wardrobe, so it probably won't come as a surprise that I was **really looking forward to seeing all those little clothes actually on his tiny body** by the end. The only thing cuter than a tiny sock is the little baby toes inside it! :) And is there a dramatic lack of fun options for boys compared to girls? Not with the right styling tricks! ;-) From my own after-the-bump wardrobe, to wearing the same clothes as my mini, to personalised accessories: **mommy fashion can be really fun!**

MY AFTER-THE-BUMP STYLING TIPS

Woohoo, fitting back into one of my favourite dresses: what a delight!
Pretty soon after giving birth, I could already fit into my wider pre-baby pieces from
my old wardrobe, but it obviously took a while for me to get my old body back – and a
couple styling tips were really useful during that period. Feel your best and wear your
post-baby bump with the same pride as ever. **A body that made a tiny person
will take some time to adapt; that's only logical!**

TIP 1 // WRAP IT UP

Whether or not it was subconsciously inspired
by swaddling our boy, my no. 1 favourite
things to wear post-baby were wraparound
skirts! Combine them with a light-weight silk
top or blouse (feels wonderful on a sensitive
skin, camouflages your postpartum tummy,
and is easy for breastfeeding!) and simply
cinch it by wrapping the skirt over it. **A pre-
shaped bag** (a wicker basket bag is perfect)
adds a bit of structure, and playful accessories
like a tasselled bracelet and gold-touched
sandal flats make the look complete!

TIP 2 // THE TOP IN A TEXTURED FABRIC

Putting together a sophisticated outfit is the
last thing you want to be doing when you just
brought a mini into the world, so keeping it
simple (and smart!) is the tip here: a sleeveless
structured beige top in a heavier fabric always
looks chique, especially in combination with
ankle-length black trousers. **Opt for a tailored
top that flares at the waist** (again, it's ideal for
camouflaging a tummy), with **a deep V-neck**
that makes it seem less sedate. A **wool variant**
is perfect in winter. You can easily cinch the
waist by tucking it into a knee-length skirt.

Add a finishing touch with your fav textured bag (an ideal way to inject a dash of colour!) and you're all set!

TIP 3 // SHIRT DRESS+

A shirt dress is one of those classics that always suits the season – winter or summer. Definitely opt for a slightly oversized version with a poppy print or brighter colour that you **cinch at the waist and allow to drape off one shoulder for a flirty accent**. Combine with a structured black/white shoulder bag and chunky slip-on shoes with refined details (that still make the cut seem feminine), like a rhinestone buckle or big bow. And in the winter, thigh-high patent leather boots are a perfect way to give your shirt dress an extra punch!

TIP 4 // A-LINE BOUDOIR DRESS

The boudoir look isn't for everyone, but it's the ideal way to distract attention from any 'flaws' you'd like to conceal. A **mini dress with an ever-flattering A-line** is a perfect way to brighten up the busy print and plumes that are characteristic of this trend. The same goes for **gold-coloured satin pumps and shaded sunnies**, preferably in a shade that's echoed in your dress. Super-fun for an evening out with your baby daddy – Moulin Rouge style!

HOW TO DO TWINNING

It's got a bit of a bad reputation: **wearing the same clothes as your mini**
– also known as 'twinning'! But I have to confess, once our mini was born,
it suddenly seemed like a **fantastic idea**. :) Anyone who can resist the appeal
of matching mini and maxi can feel free to skip this section, but I promise you that it
can be really fun when you follow these tips, whether your baby's a boy or a girl.
And otherwise it's just a good excuse to add a couple of timeless items
to your wardrobe!

FOCUS ON ACCESSOIRES

If you'd like to do a trial run to see if twinning
is right for you, accessories are the perfect way
to do it! Personally, I think there's nothing cuter than **accessories that look like a
miniature version of the adult-sized model**:
sunglasses, sun hats, caps, a tiara or rough-
and-tumble sneakers are perfect ways to subtly
reference each other's OOTD without going
hog-wild with completely matching outfits.
And you can take it just as far as you want!

GO FOR CLASSICS

The real trick to making twinning look as
casual as possible is to go for classics. And
they're super-easy to find in both baby and
adult versions! UGGs or Hunter booties,
Adidas Superstar sneakers, a Petit Bateau
sailor's jumper or Kenzo hoodie: things you'd
have in your closet anyway, so **it automatically looks a bit less contrived** – more like you
coincidentally felt like wearing identical styles
today. :)
If you'd like to try an all-matching outfit, it
can also be really fun to **play with classic
themes**: you and your mini won't necessar-

ily be wearing identical clothes, but you'll
have the same vibe, colours or prints. Like a
typical tomboy outfit consisting of a simple
white shirt, comfy jeans, black All Stars and a
baseball cap. Or: a French Rivièra outfit with a
blue-and-white striped jumper, white trousers
and camel-coloured sandals. And if you'd like
to go a little edgier: both of you can pull off
black leggings and a bomber jacket! Imagine
all this in a mini version: isn't it just darling?

**IDEAL FOR EVERYONE: HALLOWEEN AND
X-MAS**

Here's the best news: twinning is pretty much
the done thing at Halloween and Christmas –
and not just with the two of you, either! **Feel
free to involve the whole family – including
papa and the cat**. :) Matching pyjama sets are
wonderfully cheesy for the classic Christmas
cards, and he can show them off proudly to
his friends later, lol. Go as crazy as you want
for Halloween, since that's exactly what the
holiday's about. Who knows, maybe that'll
inspire you to try out some of the tips suggest-
ed above!

FROM MAMA TO BABY:
ON PERSONALISATION
AND MONOGRAMMING

Another great way to express your great love for your mini: **putting his name or initials on as many items in your wardrobe as possible!** No matter how sweet it can sometimes look, if you go overboard, you'll risk a crazy mama vibe. :)
To avoid that it's best to keep it as subtle as possible.
With these items at the top of your list, you'll definitely be set.

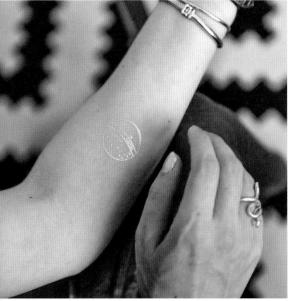

THE CLASSICS: LEATHER GOODS, BED LINENS AND BATH TOWELS

If you start personalising your favourite items by taking baby steps (ha!), leather goods are perfect! I didn't opt for a traditional diaper bag, but a **big shopper bag with smaller inside pockets** (see p. 95); that's obviously super-fun to put your baby's initials on. If you'd like to personalise your bag more flexibly, **leather labels that you can hang on your bag** are the ideal solution! And if you prefer to keep your personalised items in the privacy of your own home, there's nothing to keep you from personalising **your baby's bed linens or bath towels**. The absolute number 1 are those bath towels in animal shapes that transform your mini into the cutest duckling in the world after his bath. :)

MY FAVES
LOUIS VUITTON: pretty much the inventor of personalised leather goods
GOYARD: another classic offering beautiful big personalised shopper bags, that you can easily style even after you're no longer packing nappies

YOURS TRULY BAGS: graphic designer Kelly Howe can add the most enchanting drawings to your vintage bag upon request

MICHAEL KORS: recently started offering bag monogramming as a slightly more affordable option

JEM + BEA: a brand of baby bag approved by Vogue magazine, and of course they also offer bag personalisation; the baby backpack for nappies is definitely worth recommending, super convenient for travelling!

THE DAILY EDITED: this US-based online shop offers a wide range of personalised items, including various options for your mini (I went for the little blue backpack with a matching keyring)

LINENME: online shop with a gorgeous selection of pretty much all possible textiles for your bedroom, dining room and bathroom, with a nice range of fine hammam bath towels, linen sheets and wool blankets, all of which you can pimp according to your own preferences

DAINTY ROBES: the very cutest mini and maxi bathrobes that you can personalise with your initials or your full names

BLING: TEMPORARY TATTOOS AND DELICATE JEWELLERY

Every person who is a fan of *Sex and the City* (and who isn't?) has undoubtedly already bagged their very own Carrie necklace, which resulted in a highly personalised necklace addiction. :) Delicate jewellery with your own name on it, or the names of the people who are most precious in your life, are the modern version of the lockets people wore so they could always carry a photo of their loved ones close their hearts. And even though it might be on the cheesy side, I think it is a nice symbol, and also one that can provide a bit of bling to almost any outfit. **Whether you choose a delicate necklace, bracelet or anklet: they are all perfect for layering with chunkier accessories**, a styling trick that is 100% timeless! And if you can go a bit more playful: remember those **temporary tattoos** with Gabriel's name on that we shared together with the sweet treats we handed out after he was born? **Very nice for a party, especially when you choose a gold design** that shimmers in the sun, but isn't that dominant.

MY FAVES

TIFFANY & CO.: iconic jewellery brand with a permanent collection of bracelets and necklaces bearing initials – as a heirloom that you will cherish forever

MAYA BRENNER: my personal favourite! – the letters are permanently attached so they cannot get entangled, perfect for initials

ETSY: this online platform hosts a wide array of affordable personalised necklaces, in all possible versions (with or without rhinestones, long or short, different fonts and materials)

BABY'S FIRSTS

What is more important to get personalised than baby's firsts: his first pair of shoes, his big-boy chair at the table, his bed, his first satchel or favourite toy. **Perfect to keep as a memento, long after he has grown out of all of that! ;)**

MY FAVES

HARD TO FIND: from personalised pillows to slippers, rompers and toys – you can find it all in this online shop!

ON-THE-GO:
WHAT'S IN MY DIAPER BAG?

Putting together a compact and practical diaper bag is something that might seem easy, but is actually surprisingly hard! The very first time we took Gabriel out and about, I had packed almost half a store's worth of stuff. :) Of course I had packed too much 'what if' items that you will never ever need. After lugging ridiculous amounts of stuff around, I gradually became pickier: **the only things that were allowed in the bag were the supplies that actually make a difference**, because mama's back still needs to last a lifetime. :)

FASHION

Even though it can take up quite a bit of space, putting an **additional baby outfit** in your baby bag is always a good idea. Because you can count on it: a nappy explosion just when you want to introduce him to your dearest colleagues! A **mini-hat** is also very convenient to pack when it gets a bit nippier along the way, just like an **extra pair of socks** (they have the tendency to get kicked off along the way).

FRESHEN UP

It will probably be impossible to completely avoid getting a bit sticky when travelling with a baby, but these items will help along the way! In addition to **nappies and baby wipes**, my **on-the-go changing pad** by Théophile & Patachou has earned a permanent place in my baby bag – very convenient when you have to change your mini and there's no changing pad close by. A good **antibacterial gel** is perfect to 'wash' your hands afterwards. And on warm days, don't forget to pack your **baby sunscreen** – the Naïf version of course, it's SPF50 and part of the proceeds go to charity – and a **refreshing purifying spray** like Scented Baby Water by Linea MammaBaby.

ENTERTAINMENT

And don't forget to pack a bit of fun in your baby bag! Bringing your baby's **favourite toys and pacifier** will distract your baby along the way and can cheer up a cranky mini. Especially when he was teething, I was thrilled with the **rubber chew-toys** by Oli & Carol, made from 100% organic rubber and in lots of fun versions (for instance vegetables and fruit with names like Arnold the Avocado, Brucy the Broccoli and Kendall the Kale). :) A simple teething ring can also help, of course, especially when it has bunny ears like the Fabelab version.

FOOD & DRINKS

And talking about a cranky baby, nothing is worse for a mini (or in my case, maxi) than walking around on an empty stomach. So I never left the house without an **extra bottle, formula container** (measured out into individual servings, for instance by Beaba) and **water**. An additional **drinking cup** with water (avoid sugary drinks like fruit juice and soda!) is convenient when your baby is a bit older and starts to grab mama's beverages. And a **bib and super absorbent cotton or muslin cloth** will also help keep things tidy and clean!

Beauty & wellness

Everybody knows that cliché: a newborn baby, that means bye bye make-up and desperately hoping to find some time to grab a quick haircut after a few weeks. To put it mildly, that paints a bleak prospect, and I think it doesn't have to be that dire! Yes, you'll have less time for yourself, and for a while you'll care less about achieving that perfect cat eye, but that does not mean that you should lose sight of your own general well-being. **There are countless little things you can do to transform your baby delight into an outward glow**, and to get through those first baby months as your most beautiful self. From the most thoughtful gifts from your besties, to clever tricks to pretend you're well-rested, the most fun things to do with your mini: happy mama = happy baby, so the message is to relax and enjoy things as much as you can!

NEWBORN CHECKLIST:
THINGS YOU REALLY NEED
TO HAVE IN THE HOUSE

Contrary to what many people believe (because of my, um, extensive collection of shoes)
I am not that much of a shopper, and I will always, always, always choose quality over
quantity. So yes, I did a lot of research to avoid that typical pile of unused baby things, and
to only – or at least primarily – buy things that really make life as a new mama easier. Super
important when you've just brought a baby into this world, right? So when you're looking
for those must-have baby items right now, then let me present to you my five newborn baby
essentials that truly make a difference!

**THE MOST GORGEOUS STROLLER - MIMA
XARI**

Aaaah! The quest for the perfect stroller for
you – that is seriously hard work! :) There
are so many options out there that finding
the one seems truly impossible. But here's the
good news: if you're looking for **a stroller that
matches every outfit** (haha), that narrows
down the field significantly. When I saw that
camel leather version of the Mima Xari for the
first time, I immediately knew: this is the one!
It looks so chique and cool, and it's practical
too! It is **super solid**, so it doesn't tip over at
the slightest bump. It **grows along with your
mini**, so you can keep using it for a long time.
The only downside that I can think of is that it
is not really convenient to take along on your
travels, but there are certainly solutions for
that (see p. 130). :)

**BABY SLING - MEZAYA BABY OR
ARTIPOPPE**

It is a fact that newborn babies are always in
for extra snuggles. From day 1, Gabriel was
always excited to be really close to us; it just

had such a soothing effect on him! But as you can guess: carrying around a mini human all day can be a bit impractical, and also pretty tiring. And that's where these baby slings make all the difference. These are amongst the most stylish versions I have encountered, **available in various luxurious natural fabrics** (the linen and silk versions are my favourites) and lovely colours that match almost any outfit (it's a matter of keeping it stylish :)). And these slings are also **easy to use**, crucial for all exhausted new mamas and papas!

ORGANIC COTTON BABY SLEEPING NEST – BABYNEST

This baby sleeping nest is as simple as it is genius, and because I use it so much, I immediately bought it in two different colours. When your baby is still a real mini, it will keep him safe and comfy in his seemingly huge bed. One always remains permanently in Gabriel's bed at home, and we take the other nest with us when we visit friends or family where it turns **any seat or large soft surface into a nice and cosy bed.** Super practical!

HIGH CHAIR - STOKKE STEPS

The best thing about this chair is that your baby can join you at the table, no matter how small he is. As a born foodie, the ritual of sitting down for dinner was something I was looking forward to most. Turns out it's also **good to familiarise your baby with the principle of dinner time from the start**, and to offer a nice quiet atmosphere to finally taste his first solid food. When he sees mama and papa enjoy so many delicious foods, he is bound to want to copy that quickly as well! :)

RELAX SEAT - 4MOMS MAMAROO

I had already heard so many good things about this seat, and Gabriel adores it as well! You can choose between **various movement settings and soothing musics** (the kangaroo bounce and heartbeat tune are the most popular over here :)). And yep, this seat has already managed to prevent a few serious crying fits. Plus, the subtle white-and-grey design looks great in your interior – a welcome change from the most super colourful baby items!

COZY SLEEPING BAG - THÉOPHILE & PATACHOU

From the very start, it was clear that our baby boy would be travelling a lot. So, just like his baby nest, this sleeping bag is used all the time! It is pretty much the easiest item to carry along; the sleeping bag is **nice and soft and warm, but also reasonably lightweight.** The flared shape ensures that your baby will still have sufficient space to move his little legs, while ensuring he has a nice snuggly feeling – ever so important for a lovely night's sleep (or at least a couple of hours :)). Of course I also like the clean classic design that goes so well with our Théophile & Patachou furniture (see previously). Couldn't be better!

THE 5 NOT-THAT-OBVIOUS PRESENTS EVERY NEW MOMMY SECRETLY WANTS

It is obvious that your baby will be the centre of attention during those first post-birth visits, and that most of the presents from your friends and family will focus on your mini-superstar (also because of your baby registry, of course). But when one of my dearest friends stopped by with a week's supply of home-made meals and snacks, it felt like **one of the most caring and thoughtful gifts we received.** So, when you are also looking for that one thing that will make your nappy-swamped bestie feel truly special... then these tips will set you on the right track - and some of them aren't even material!

CAPTURING THOSE PRECIOUS FIRST MONTHS

FUJIFILM INSTAX MINI INSTANT CAMERA
Despite the fact that documenting my life is an important part of my job, I am still surprised how easily you forget to capture those first few months, in between all those sleepless nights and nappies. You are so preoccupied with finding a new rhythm that you might almost forget to take photographs of your mini, who changes so much almost every day! Until you're a few months down the road and you realise that your newborn has suddenly and inexplicably gotten so huge! **If you want to document your baby from the very start in a special (non-phone :)) way**, an updated version of the traditional Polaroid camera is simply perfect. For instant fun that you'll

cherish forever, since framing the cutest photo is absolutely vital!

DECADENT HEALTHY TREAT
CHOCOLATE AND STRAWBERRIES
Let's be fair: getting back to your pre-baby weight is hard work, and probably the last thing you want to get started on while you're still busy finding your way during those first few months. So a fruity snack that feels decadent (and sexy!) is exactly what you need on those days when your baby never seems to stop crying and the nights are extra short. :) **Chocolate-dipped strawberries (frozen if necessary during the winter months, when it's impossible to find fresh ones!) are easy to make at home**, and perfect to bring along in a lovely box-with-a-bow – with a warm hug and a stuffed animal, of course!

THE WAY TO THEIR HEART IS...
HOME-MADE YUMMY DINNERS
And speaking about food: a week's supply of home-made meals is about the best possible gift for any new mama! And if you really want to go full Nigella Lawson: **include an ingredient list and short instructions with each meal**, so it's truly just a matter of enjoyment, with zero stress.

CHOCOLATE CHIP AND PEANUT COOKIES
For 25 cookies
· 80 g unsalted butter, at room temperature
· 150 g coconut oil
· 250 g crunchy peanut butter
· 130 g cane sugar
· 120 g brown sugar
· 2 large eggs
· 350 g flour
· 2 teaspoons of baking powder

optional: coarse sea salt, to sprinkle on the cookies before they go into the oven

Mix butter, coconut oil, peanut butter and sugar in a bowl and add the eggs. Sift the flour and baking powder into another bowl and add it to the butter mixture. Put the dough in the refrigerator for 1 hour.
Next make some 2-3 cm balls from that dough that you can easily pop in the freezer! In the mood for fresh cookies? Just put a number of these balls on a baking tray covered with grease-proof baking paper and put it in a pre-heated oven at 180 °C. Bake for approximately 10 minutes, *et voilà!*

MASSAGE AT HOME
TREATWELL.BE
Of all the immaterial presents, a massage is absolutely in my top 3 – and maybe everyone's! But considering that travelling with a baby is close to a small relocation, an at-home massage contributes to that feeling of total relaxation; you do not need to organise anything, just relax for a couple of hours... That completely sorts your week!

THE ULTIMATE ME-TIME
A BABYSITTER
The dream of any new mama: an afternoon of pure me-time. Offering to babysit will definitely be appreciated! I vividly recall how much impact it had on me to just go out in the city centre for a couple of hours; shop a bit, spotting some people with cake and tea, finding inspiration in my favourite magazines... And then head back home quickly, because you missed your mini sooo much! :)

3 EASY CHEAT SLEEP BEAUTY TRICKS
TO INSTANTLY LOOK AWAKE

I can still remember my face (and general state of mind :)) during those first few months with our newborn baby: somewhere between blissfully happy, extremely exhausted and a little desperate. As much as I was used to an irregular lifestyle and nights with little sleep, this was still a different experience. That means it was time to brush up on my favourite beauty tricks to look (more) awake again in a jiffy!

IT'S IN YOUR EYES
VERSO REVIVING EYE MASK
A tissue mask placed on your face like a second skin always looks a bit dramatic, but once you see **how much effect this eye mask has on your entire face,** I guarantee you'll be sold! You place the pre-shaped gel pads under your eyes for 20 minutes. After that, gently massage any gel that was not absorbed into your skin with your fingers, immediately after removing the pads. The result is a super hydrated skin and fewer fine lines around your eyes. During an extended period of less sleep, you can use this twice a week, but for me just using it once per month already made a huge difference!

THINK GOLD & GLOSSY
MAC DAZZLESHADOW IN 'I LIKE 2 WATCH'
AND STUDIO EYE GLOSS
It's no coincidence that this is still one of the most popular tricks ever: a dash of gold-coloured highlighter at the inner corner of your eye! Choose a yellowish gold (instead of reddish copper) to get the freshest effect, and dab it to ensure that it stays in place nicely. And for those of you who can use an additional boost: a more recent interpretation of the ever-fresh effect of a bit of shine is eye gloss, a shiny eye shadow that you apply on your eyelid in one single layer. For that perfect awake look – a runway favourite!

DO NOT USE A POWDER FINISH
MAC STROBE CREAM
It's a simple fact that a hydrated, slightly glossy skin will always look fresher than a powdered finish. **So stick to your BB cream or foundation, which you can easily mix with some day cream for additional hydration.** Or use a 2-in-1 version like the strobe cream by MAC for an even faster just-right effect!

MONDAY MORNING WITH A BABY:
MY FAVOURITE TIPS FOR AIR-DRIED HAIR

Monday morning: not exactly everyone's favourite moment of the week. Realising that yesterday's last glass of red wine was actually not such a good idea, just plain stuck about what to wear for that important meeting, not to mention the prospect of endless traffic jams, sudden downpours and way too short lunches. Yiiiiikes. Add an inexplicably cranky baby to that and your look is probably the last thing you want to work on today. Introducing: air-dried hair! But doesn't abandoning your hair-dryer guarantee frizzy, fluffy hair? Absolutely not, with these tips!

NO SHAMPOO ON THE LOCKS

Whether you have long or shorter hair, avoid applying extra shampoo to the locks of your hair (which is everything not touching your scalp). Since shampoo is designed to get your hair clean, it generally also has a dehydrating effect. **That means you need to focus on the hair that is closest to your scalp.** Which is of course the part that could really use a good scrub. And **trust that the rest of your hair will also get washed when rinsing out** the shampoo you put on the top of your head. Easy, isn't it?

MICROFIBRE TOWEL

AQUIS LISSE LUXURY HAIR TOWEL

It may sound funny, but preventing frizzy or fuzzy hair starts first and foremost with... your towel! The type of towel that you use to dry your hair right after washing has a huge effect on frizz, because when you rub it too dry (using a classic towel and upward movements) it will frizz your hair regardless. **That is why you should only squeeze your hair once or twice and rub a good absorbing microfibre towel over your hair until most of the water has been absorbed.** And here is the most ironic fact: the 100% cotton cloth nappies that you can easily find in bigger retail chains are perfect for this!

COMB YOUR HAIR INSTEAD OF BRUSHING IT

MASON PEARSON RAKE COMB C7

Your hair is at its most vulnerable when it is wet or damp, so it's not a good idea to brush it in that state. The fine bristles of a brush in combination with the rough 'tugging movement' to pull it through your hair will make it go all frizzy. **So just use your fingers or a wide tooth comb and start with the ends of your hair** (so definitely not on top, in order to avoid excessive pulling). Once your hair is a bit drier, then you can always opt to brush it carefully if it needs a bit more work.

LEAVE-IN CONDITIONER

KIEHL'S DAMAGE REPAIRING & REHYDRATING LEAVE-IN TREATMENT

If you have hair that easily frizzes and is susceptible to dry ends, a leave-in conditioner that you apply to moist hair without rinsing it out is a must-have. **Make sure you do not use too much,** because that can also cause frizz, **and carefully apply it to the locks of your hair** before combing (using a comb or fingers).

BRAID IT

If you want to add some more texture to your hair as well as prevent frizz – because it will also improve the absorption of the hydrating products you just put in – braiding your moist hair is a super-awesome idea! Use a loose version and seamless hair elastic to avoid crimp marks from the twists, and unbraid your hair as soon as it's almost completely dry. Shake out your natural waves and add a dab of nutrient-rich hair cream if necessary. And you're all set!

THE CUTEST BABY-MAMA NIGHT-TIME RITUALS ARE CREATED LIKE THIS

I had always been very curious how we would integrate our little baby into our irregular (alright, chaotic :)) lifestyle. Our work is literally our life, and no two days are the same: it's lovely in the sense that it never feels like a job, but possibly not ideal for creating that sense of structure that children famously need so much. I must admit I was a bit rattled at first, but as these things go, that feeling disappeared completely once our boy had arrived. Of course babies do have their own rhythms (sleeping, eating, sleeping, eating :)) but that can be fun as well, and a regular evening routine can even help your baby fall asleep faster and more soundly – that makes it ideal to guarantee that feeling of 'home' (and therefore a good night's rest) even when you are travelling!

STEP 1

BATHING AND THE LAST BOTTLE OF THE DAY

Most babies love a good splashing session, so starting your evening ritual with a bath is definitely a good idea. **The warm water will relax your mini at any rate**, and if you notice that they still have too much energy, it is also a good moment to **play together for a while** – rubber duckies are just plain brilliant. :) A hungry baby will have trouble falling asleep, so after bathing it is time for the baby's last bottle of the day. **Always feed your baby in the same tranquil place**, for instance the nursery, so he will recognise that final bottle of the day and realise that it is time to go to bed.

STEP 2

BEDTIME STORY, MINI MASSAGE AND A LULLABY

No matter how small your baby is, 'reading' a book is always fun, and the perfect way for your mini to learn something along the way –how to distinguish bright colours, imitate animals or learn new words. Disregard the crackling and other noisy or interactive books; instead, choose the **classic baby's-first-word books or stories**. During reading or right

after, you can gently massage your baby's legs, back, arms and belly to help their **body relax and offset any growing pains.** Even just gently rubbing their bellies will have a very soothing effect! And yup, for the people who like it (and can do it ;)), it is time to sing a lullaby! **One of the most soothing things for your mini is still mama's voice.** And the good news is: there is not a baby in the world who can tell when you sing off-key! :) When your baby is a little older and starts to babble, the **goodnight moon ritual** is a good alternative: you go around the baby room to say goodnight to all their favourite stuffed animals and other objects. And it will be even more fun when you tell little stories as you go!

STEP 3

NIGHT-LIGHT ON WITH A BIT OF MUSIC
Don't like sleeping in a completely quiet, pitch-dark room? Chances are your mini won't enjoy it either! So buy a cute night light (I show a few of my favourites on p. 111) and a teddy bear or dangling mobile with soft children's music and switch them on just before you put your baby to bed. Now it is really time to sleep – just one more kiss and nighty night!

HUSH BABY HUSH:
HOW TO TURN MINI-NIGHTS
INTO MAXI-NIGHTS

One thing I had already in common with our mini: babies are very focused on sensory input. Since everything is still developing, all stimuli – scents, colours, sounds, tastes and textures – are experienced 100% and unfiltered, which can be quite overwhelming. But here is the good news: you can 'manipulate' that oversensitivity, because someone who is sensitive to negative input is just as susceptible to happy sensory triggers. And that's exactly what you can use to turn those infamous mini-nights into maxi-nights (or as close as possible)!

SMELL: CALMING PILLOW SPRAY
SUSANNE KAUFMANN
People who are (over)sensitive are guaranteed to have them: scent memories! Lavender always takes me back to warm summer vacations in the south of France, together with my family: a wonderful mix of baguettes, the ocean, popsicles, petanque, sun-burned shoulders and chirping crickets. Small wonder that **this organic spray with a lavender base and fresh**

orange oil has such an instant calming effect. That also proved the case with our mini. A quick spray on his blankets fifteen minutes before bedtime and ... sweet dreams!

HEAR: SLEEP SHEEP
CLOUD B

This 'miracle sheep' (also available as a giraffe :)) plays the most soothing natural sounds, which will comfort any sad baby and slowly rock it back to sleep. Due to the unprecedented success of the original version, this gadget is now also available as an on-the-go version to attach to the stroller – for the best naps during the day!

SEE: NIGHT STAND
A LITTLE LOVELY COMPANY

Nothing is scarier than a dark room, so a small, dim night-light is vital in every nursery. And because some things are better when they are cute, you shouldn't hesitate to choose a kitsch but oh so sweet pastel-coloured mini-dinosaur, unicorn, cloud or ghost :).

FEEL: SWADDLING CLOTHES
NATURE BABY

I already mentioned it previously: swaddling your baby may feel a bit odd (who would like lying in bed like a mummy??) but if you realise that **your belly** – the only environment your mini was familiar with before – **was not particularly spacious either, you can probably imagine the soothing effect.** Nowadays you can find swaddling clothes in just about any baby store, but my favourites are the ones from Francis & Henry, and the 100% natural ones by Nature Baby, in a soft organic merino wool, cotton or muslin version, and of course equally suitable to use as a blanket.

EXTRA: SWADDLING FOR DUMMIES
STEP 1: Lay out your cloth and fold one corner to the centre, creating a triangle. Place your baby in the centre of the triangle, with his shoulders just below the edge of the cloth.
STEP 2: Hold one arm down and gently fold one side of the cloth over it.
STEP 3: Tuck the cloth under your baby's body (between the arm and the sides), ensuring that the cloth is snug.
STEP 4: Fold the bottom of the cloth up, which will put the baby's legs in a 'pouch', and tuck the cloth in.
STEP 5: Finally, hold the other arm down, fold the final side of the cloth over it and tuck it in. Your baby's own weight should keep the cloth in place, so make sure that your swaddling cloth is big enough to tuck under your baby's body.

TASTE: DETOX TEA
SUSANNE KAUFMANN

Tea is one of my perpetual obsessions, and as soon as I knew the ingredients of this purifying version, I was sold immediately: mint, apple, verbena, rose hip and fennel are a selection of some of the most yummy organic herbs and fruits (theine-free of course) which will **help your body relax after a stressful day.** When you're breastfeeding, your newborn baby can enjoy it indirectly, and from 6-8 months it offers a nice occasional alternative to water.

OUR 3 BASIC PARENTING RULES

No matter how long you have been together and how well you have prepared for your mini's arrival, **being a mama and papa is something you mostly learn along the way.** And it's best not to worry about it too much. :) Chances are good – since both of you share the same values in life (after all, you are a couple and all that ;)) – that you also share the same ideas about raising your baby. Now it is not as if Marcio and I had prepared a strategic plan in advance, but now that our boy is a bit bigger, we have established 3 main criteria that have helped us in supporting each other as parents.

TEAM SPIRIT

This may seem obvious, but one of the biggest pitfalls for young first-time parents is the good cop/bad cop phenomenon: **one parent vetoes or disapproves of something, while the other says it's fine.** Besides being very inefficient,

it is also simply confusing: which side should your mini choose; who should he believe? Even when you do not always agree with the things that your baby daddy disapproves of, it is often better not to argue in the presence of your baby. A matter of maintaining credibility for both of you. Do approach him about it at a later time, and try to align things to accommodate both your viewpoints. That way your mini knows: when mama says no, there is no use in trying to find sympathy from papa.

BE A COUPLE

Making time for yourself as a couple is not always easy when you have a tiny person who keeps you up all night and is also super cute as well, and therefore very good at demanding every bit of your attention. But remember how important it was to focus on the two of you during your babymoon? Well, that still applies once your baby has arrived. I can still clearly remember our very first trip abroad without Gabriel, how hard it was to leave him with his grandma and grandpa (who were of course sooo enthusiastic about that :)), but **in hindsight those 2 days and 1 wonderfully long night were very refreshing.** And when there is no short-term chance for a weekend getaway,

you can always **just organise a romantic date night at home.** Because that is the big benefit of babies: they go to bed so early that you'll still have the whole evening to yourselves!

GROWING AS A FAMILY

People often wonder what the secret is of our 10-year relationship. There are several, but one of the most important is definitely that Marcio and I have always made a point of growing together. People evolve and change (and that is a good thing too!) and the biggest challenge lies in **finding each other again in every phase of life. Creating as many memories as possible together** will help tremendously with that; when you're in a less wonderful period, you can fall back on the good times and immediately remember why it pays to make your relationship work. And that also applies to the rest of the family: nothing creates such a strong connection as **trying new things out together**, extending your boundaries and doing things that may feel scary at first. If you're wondering whether you should go on that trip abroad with your mini: go for it! It will help your family grow closer.

BABY DATES:
QUALITY TIME WITH YOUR MINI

Remember how I wondered before our baby arrived how we would fit him into our lives? When I mentioned this to a friend in a slightly panicky tone (because your besties have the very best baby advice, as I have already stated before! :)), she gave me this super easy but absolute genius tip: **imagine your baby while you are doing specific things together.** It helped immensely to make the whole baby-mama story less abstract and to look forward to the little but oh so important experiences we would soon share – which is of course so much more than just feeding him and rocking him to sleep. :) So if you are wondering how to spend quality time with a tiny person who is not that communicative yet but sooooo curious: let me present to you my list of favourites!

SUNDAY CITY BRUNCH

I always loved this picture: mama, papa and kids out on a Sunday to enjoy a big yummy brunch. :) Raising a baby in the city might not always be ideal, but it is just perfect for brunch: there are so many options, so many new places and so many different dishes to try. It is a fun way to **familiarise your mini with new flavours** of things you wouldn't necessarily make yourself at home. And since brunch is generally considered a family activity, chances are good that your mini will be welcomed

with open arms. After all, it is also a fun ritual which you can repeat every week without getting boring, which will be something your kiddo will remember fondly in the future...

PICNIC IN THE PARK

Another simple yet wonderful city activity with your family is a picnic in the park! It was one of our favourites with our newborn baby. It was a way for us to get some fresh air and get our mini distracted when he was a bit grumpy. :) **Put on your favourite Hollywood road trip outfit** (a loose chiffon dress, matching slippers, multi-coloured scarf in your hair and white-rimmed cat's-eye sunglasses perched on your nose), **take along some easy summer snacks** (watermelon!), and you're ready for a wonderful afternoon of gazing at clouds and guessing animals!

TEXTURE TIME: DIY PLAYDOUGH & GUESS THE ANIMAL

Even though it may not seem like it when he eats and sleeps so much, the baby phase is specifically about learning lots. Everything is still new, free to be discovered and to leave an impression, and all of it contributes to your baby's development. So if there is one time to focus on that, it is now! And in addition to dancing, singing and 'reading' books, discovering new textures is one of the most important things you can teach your baby at a very early age, and of course also the perfect way to make him a mini-fashion baby ;) **Tactile books with various types of animal fur** help baby learn his first words as well, and if you have time for a more hands-on approach: **what could be more fun than an afternoon messing around with home-made playdough?!** (such nostalgia...)

DIY PLAYDOUGH

· 130 g flour
· 75 g salt
· 230 ml water
· 1 teaspoon olive oil
· 3 teaspoon lemon juice
optional: a few drops of beet juice, carrot juice or blueberry juice or a pinch of cocoa powder, matcha powder or turmeric powder

Put all the ingredients in a pan and simmer it on low heat for a while until it turns into a lump of dough. You could also divide the dough up and make different colours by adding the natural colours listed above. Save in an airtight jar so your playdough will not dry out. A miniature rolling pin and some cookie cutters, and dough away!

TASTE TOGETHER

And while we are on the subject of home-made things: familiarising your baby with different types of flavours at an early age is a great idea, especially if you want him to be just as much as a foodie as his mama! :) Starting at six months, your mini can also taste other things in addition to his bottles, and there are more exciting choices than just the classic fruit and veggie mash! Focus on **ingredients with bright colours** to make it extra fun and make sure to also try out some **unexpected combinations**; a matter of familiarising with as many **different types of flavours** as possible, and avoid the risk of him turning into a picky eater. More of my (and Gabriel's :)) favourite baby recipes are provided on p. 118!

CHEAT FOOD:
1-MINUTE HEALTHY SNACKS
THAT YOUR BABY WILL TRULY LOVE

When I couldn't even stand smelling any food during the first months of my pregnancy, let alone keeping it down, there was a moment when I was seriously thinking: will this baby ever be able to love food? That seemed a big problem for me at the time, because as a real foodie, I would probably have serious problems empathising with a difficult eater – baby or not. :) And even though Gabriel eats just about anything so far, I keep making these super easy yummy nutritious snacks that no mini can resist over and over again, because... mama is a fan too!

FROZEN BANANA YOGHURT STICKS

Mash a banana, mix it with soy or coconut yoghurt until it's a liquid mixture, pour it into pre-made ice pop moulds, and freeze them until they are solid enough to slip out easily.

SWEET POTATO CHIPS

Cut a sweet potato into thin slices, arrange them in a casserole greased with olive oil, season it with sea salt, pepper, sesame seeds and flaked almonds. Roast them until they are all shrivelled up and crispy (about 10 minutes, depending on your oven and the thickness of the slices).

FRUIT KABOBS

Slice your favourite fruit into small pieces (pineapple, currants, raspberries, apples and grapes are always a hit!) and put them in random order on a plastic skewer with rounded tips until you have a colourful, yummy fruit kabob.

AVOCADO AND FETA MASH

Mash an avocado and add a little olive oil to it to soften it up. Add a bit of soft crumbled feta as well as some pepper and salt and mix it thoroughly.

APPLE SLICES WITH PEANUT BUTTER

Slice a big apple into four pieces and divide each quarter into small slices. Cover the slices with a layer of peanut butter (or almond butter) and add a finishing touch by sprinkling them with some chia seeds.

FRIED BANANA WITH CINNAMON AND COCONUT

Heat some olive oil in a pan. Fry semi-ripe slices of banana two minutes on each side and sprinkle them with cinnamon and coconut flakes.

SCRAMBLED EGG WITH COTTAGE CHEESE AND ROASTED BELL PEPPER

Beat one egg with a bit of milk, pepper, salt and chopped parsley, pour it into a frying pan, and add a spoon-full of cottage cheese and pieces of roasted bell pepper to the mixture.

FRESH PITA WITH HUMMUS AND CHERRY TOMATOES

Add chickpeas, sesame paste, olive oil, water, pepper and salt into the blender and blend it until it is smooth. Spread it on a pita and add sliced cherry tomatoes.

FAMILY TRADITIONS:
HOW DO YOU CELEBRATE THEM IN STYLE?

Each mama has her own specific extra special things that she really wants to share with her mini; those sweet family rituals take you back to your childhood and are passed on from grandma to mama to baby, now until forever. You know, those timeless traditions that you share with each other year after year, that give you an authentic family feeling which will never, ever feel dated. Because no matter how many Instagrams and Snapchats and new cool superstars there may be, searching for chocolate eggs or decorating the Christmas tree together is simply better than anything. And yup, **traditions demand clichés, but that does not mean that you cannot add your personal touch to it**. An entire year celebrating the most wonderful family traditions (and matching souvenirs that you can keep up with): this is how you do it!

JAN/FEB OH BABY BABY: HAPPY VALENTINE'S DAY!

Celebrating Valentine's: whether or not you're a fan, no one can ever object to opening up the concept and celebrating love. And what better company on Valentine's than your love baby? So, when you are kind of done with the slightly forced candlelight dinners (and finding the perfect Valentine's gift: yikes!), **your mini is the perfect Valentine**. :) Make it a lovely luxurious day, with all your favourite cakes, wonderfully long splash sessions in the tub, and mini massages.

FOREVER & EVER: LOVE LETTER 2.0

If you can't be a little cheesy on Valentine's Day, when can you? A super fun way to document your annual day of love is... **writing an old-fashioned love letter, addressed to your mini of course**! In other words: summarise all the things that make you love him so much at the moment – from the sweetest things he does to the craziest habits. Even though it might seem now like you'll never forget these things, in 10 years you'll be glad you wrote them down. And you will have an annual selfie of the both of you with lipstick kisses (so cheesy ;)) which you can then give to dad. This will definitely be the only Valentine's gift he will be looking forward to every year. Love, love, love!

MARCH/APRIL EASTER EGG HUNT

Anyone who grows up in the country of chocolate takes Easter very seriously, including a cool scavenger hunt for tons of Easter eggs, and eating just a tad more chocolate than your stomach can handle for days on end – but who cares? It's only Easter once per year, so you should do it right!

Hiding things and looking for them is something that every mini loves, because it is such an adventure! And when it is also chocolate figurines, then....well, let's just say that it is hard to fall asleep on the day before Easter. :) And that applies to kids as well as to mama and papa, who need to step up their game as designated Easter bunnies to create a memorable chocolate paradise. Start by **picking out a nice green spot** which has plenty of places to hide eggs, and of course that spot has to be child-friendly. If you don't have a garden, then a city park or forest will serve just as well. That requires a bit more organisation, so it could be a good idea to share the workload with friends who have kids. Step 2 may sound a little neurotic, but you will be glad that you have done it: **make a map which shows the hiding places of all the treats,** to avoid half the treats being left behind simply because no one remembers where they were. That would be a waste of your time and effort, and the kids would be so disappointed! When your little Easter egg hunters are still young, it is best to choose **chocolates in brightly coloured wrappers,** which will make them easier to spot.

FOREVER & EVER: EASTER BASKET WITH DIY PASTEL EGGS

If you want to make your mini's annual Easter egg hunt extra special, make your very own personalised wicker basket. Which you can also use as a keepsake every year! Add a few cute extras: **confetti, water balloons** (perfect entertainment for an après-hunt water balloon fight!), **home-made cookies, spring flower seeds to plant with your mini...** And when your kid is a little older, it is also super fun to fill the basket with **little things to create these lovely pastel eggs yourself**: for pink

eggs, you can add beets, which you can boil to make naturally coloured red water. Once it has cooled a bit, you can make the colour permanent with a bit of white wine vinegar. Place your hard-boiled eggs in the water until they have the colour you want and dry them carefully. Use the same process for light blue eggs, this time using a bit of red cabbage. A full day of Easter fun guaranteed!

MAY/JUNE MOTHER'S DAY

Your first Mother's Day is an occasion that you'll never forget! It almost feels like a second birthday, but without all the pressure of organising a party and receiving 1001 birthday wishes – sounds perfect, right? It is fun to come up with a few activities which you can engage in every year to make that day extra special: **breakfast in bed with the entire family, a bit of shopping** to get those heels that have been on your wish list for a while, eating pastries in the city... This is your day!

FOREVER & EVER: HANDPRINTS IN CLAY

I have no idea if everyone still does this, but when we were little it was absolutely one of the most beloved Mother's Day gifts: a print of our mini's hands in clay! Suitable for any budget, absolutely awesome to do (young or old, who doesn't like messing with clay? :)) and a super cute memento which will warm any mama's heart. **So lovely to line up all of those hands after a couple of years and gaze in sheer amazement at how those hands could ever have been that tiny.** A classic, and with good reason!

JULY/AUG HI SUMMER: FAMILY HOLIDAYS

The most beautiful childhood memories I have are the ones of our family holidays in the

south of France: building sand castles with my brother all day long, our feet in the hot sand, only eating ice creams and baguettes, and that dazzling and delicious scent of salty sea water and fresh lavender sachets in our sleeping rooms – take me back! **I am sure that this is where I picked up my travel bug, my urge to keep discovering new places around the world.** And that is something that I'd love to pass on to our mini. Travelling has always been an important (and lovely!) part of my work, but an annual trip with a 100% focus

on just our family is absolutely high on my priority list (and more of my favourite tips to travel with a baby can be found on p. 128 in the book!).

FOREVER & EVER: BEACH BUM MEMORIES
The ultimate way to document your family holidays is of course by taking as many pictures as possible! There is nothing cuter than a mini swimsuit with little legs covered in sand, or a blissful mini with a dripping ice cream cone. :) And to have that holiday feeling all

year long: **have the best of your photos turned into a calendar or memory game.** The Artifact Uprising online shop, appropriately established by two sisters, makes the most beautiful options! And that also makes it a fun way to remember all the family members who shared in the holiday fun, even the ones that live a bit further away...

SEPT/OCT HALLOWEEN

Halloween may originally come from the USA, but when our mini arrived, I suddenly realised why it has also become so popular in Europe. Because making delicious pumpkin pie together and using the leftovers to create scary lanterns, and looking for twinned scary costumes, is just so much fun! And any excuse to get some candy during those long winter months is great, right?

FOREVER & EVER: SCARY COSTUMES

Dressing up a baby is one of the most fun things a mama can do. :) **Just like making super-high mini ponytails, it is one of those things which you know will end one day, so you might as well go for it 100%,** while your mini is still okay to go through life as a fluffy unicorn for one day. People who remember those framed baby animals in the baby room will not be surprised that they also make by far my favourite Halloween costumes for babies. The Pottery Barn Kids online shop, which offers international shipping, has the cutest! A woolly white rabbit, an absurdly cute lion cub or a tiny shark: why can't we have Halloween more often?

NOV/DEC HAPPY HOLIDAYS!

Of all the months of the year, those last few weeks towards the end of the year are the perfect time to spend as much time as possible with your family, and simply **go for all the X-mas clichés** you can! All December long, getting up with Christmas carols (which you can all sing along to), personalised Christmas stockings stuffed to the toe with presents, decorating your kitschy, over-the-top Christmas tree and making countless gingerbread biscuits: all things to really look forward to. Memories that you'd love to put in a box and carry with you the rest of the year.

FOREVER & EVER: FAMILY X-MAS CARD

The best way to close the year is by sending traditional Christmas cards. It is such a sweet tradition, and believe me, once you have a baby, you want nothing more than to immortalise your happy family and send that picture to your most beloved friends and family, no matter how cliché it is. So yes, **grab those matching flannel plaid PJs and the homemade wool cap for the cat or dog,** stand in front of the Christmas tree and smile! It's a wonderful way to document the evolution of your family, and at the same time you will have the perfect super embarrassing pictures to show to your mini's very first love :)

QUE?
5 TIPS TO RAISE A MULTI-LINGUAL BABY

When Marcio and I discovered that we were expecting a baby, we immediately knew: this will truly be a fifty-fifty baby! We both believed it would be beneficial if he would get the best of two completely different cultures. It goes without saying that we wanted to pass on the blend of Belgian deliberation and Brazilian spirit that make mama and papa such a good team (ahem ;)).
He would grow up in Belgium, but his name would indicate his Brazilian origin
(a matter of choosing something that would sound nice with his papa's last name, Bastos).
And if the hyperactivity in my belly was any indication of his character, then inheriting
the Brazilian joie de vivre was guaranteed.
And then we were suddenly confronted with the practical side: what about the language? Marcio and I were used to speaking English with each other, but both of us considered it important that the baby would speak our respective native languages of Portuguese and Dutch; a matter of giving him a full-fledged place in our families, as well as a clear connection to his roots, of course. But how? After countless stays in Brazil and a couple of immersive lessons, my command of the Portuguese language still remained limited to smoothly ordering food (priorities!).
Would it also be that hard for a mini? It proved less difficult than expected,
as long as you remember a few things!

TALK THAT TALK

Remember how babies can still whoop in sheer delight after the 200th time of doing peekaboo just like the very first time? Yup, they love repetition and patterns that help them to divide that completely new world filled with impressions and people and shapes and colours and smells into bite-size pieces that are comprehensible to their mini-brains. And the same applies to learning a new language: whether it is just one or several, **it all revolves around talking a lot and repeatedly with your baby to familiarise him with the sounds.** Even when you think that he does not understand a single thing: keep on talking to him as much as you can and preferably also **keep on making eye contact** so he can follow your mouth. Seeing, copying, mastering: it is as simple as that!

GO BIG

Talking with your mini in different languages is most certainly the basis for teaching him various languages, but when you truly want to aim for a solid working knowledge, you need to go beyond that: **various forms of entertainment like singing songs, watching TV and reading books also have a huge impact on linguistic development.** When you know that your child will be in contact with a certain language for the majority of his life (at school or in his immediate surroundings), then it is best to focus on the other language at home in the child's exposure to entertainment. Incorporate this as much as possible into your baby's daily routine: reading a Brazilian book or singing a lullaby as part of his evening routine will already have a huge impact, and don't underestimate the effect of background music either.

THE MORE THE MERRIER

It is always best to learn a language in its original habitat, so if you have the opportunity to immerse your baby in the language which he is least in contact with during the year (that is always inevitably the case): go for it! An extended holiday in Brazil, where he can follow the cheerful chatter of his grandma and aunts, will 'train' him every year until he is able to talk as easily as they can and can order food for his mama in fluent Portuguese. :)

Travel

MY ULTIMATE TIPS FOR TRAVELLING WITH A MINI

Even though it did not feel like it at that time, travelling with a rounded tummy was actually nothing more than a warm-up for the real thing: going on the road with your baby! Apart from the fact that you need to lug around half a supermarket, babies are also not that flexible: when they're upset, hungry or sleepy, instant action needs to be taken, even when you have been stuck in traffic for 3 hours, the entire plane needs to be vacated due to engine trouble (why?), or your grumpy neighbour in the train to London has already scowled at you countless times. But as one does, you learn from your mistakes (especially when they are extra embarrassing!). And after a few long flights and more than a couple of public crying fits, we faithfully stick to these tips, because **even though it takes some practice to turn your mini into a baby explorer, it is most assuredly well worth it!**

5 THINGS YOU'LL NEED
WHEN TRAVELLING WITH A BABY

Discovering new pieces of the world has always been an important part of my life, and before
Gabriel was born I mostly used to dream about picture-perfect trips where he was quietly
enjoying his new environment – no public scenes or stained outfits in sight. :)
Fast-forward to his first trip to Paris when he was 5,5 months old. It was immediately clear that
travelling with a mini went hand in hand with lots of lugging stuff around.
So yep, out of all the baby purchases I made, the ones that made our beloved trips a whole lot
easier were certainly the best investments. If you're planning a family trip of your own,
then these are the 5 things you will need when travelling with a baby!

SUPER-COMPACT STROLLER – BABYZEN YOYO

If you ever make just one single travel-friendly
purchase, let it be this super-compact stroller.
No matter how happy I am with my beautiful
Mima Xari, it did not seem very suitable to
take with me on my travels. Someone recom-
mended the Babyzen stroller to me as one of
the most light-weight strollers out there, and
it did not disappoint me at all! **In no time,
you can transform it into a compact package
that is perfect for checking in at the airport**,
and even though you do need to pay a bit of
attention on the streets (it tips easily because
it is really very light), it is just super practical
and cute, so therefore a winner!

FOLDABLE TRAVEL BED – AEROMOOV

Another item that is so wonderfully compact
and easily transforms into a comfy bed! What
I find most convenient about this item is that
**its rectangular shape means it can not only
serve as a bed, but just as easily as a play-
ground**, once your mini gets older. It's simple
and safe, and 100% no fuss.

2-IN-1 CAR SEAT/STROLLER
SIMPLE PARENTING DOONA

When we went to Paris for the first time with the three of us, we hadn't foreseen that Gabriel would already have outgrown his baby-car seat. He couldn't sit straight on his own yet (obviously!), so this 2-in-1 toddler-car seat/stroller was a real lifesaver! He's perfect to bring with you on long car rides, so you don't have to wake your mini all the time.

MUSICAL SHEEP - EASIDREAM

I had already heard plenty of good things about this fluffy sheep before Gabriel was even born. Besides the fact that it is soft and cuddly, it also has a double soothing effect with a **soft pink light and soothing noises** (including a heartbeat, waterfall, harp and ahem, vacuum cleaner :)). It is also easy to carry with you and it will make your mini feel at home, wherever you are.

EXTRA LONG SLEEPING BAG - BABY BITES

With his long legs, Gabriel had soon outgrown his first sleeping bag, so this cute shark from Baby Bites (98 cm long!) was the perfect addition to our baby travel items. It is soft and practical, 100% cotton and **can also be used in the stroller** to keep your mini nice and warm when travelling. And fair is fair: it also instantly brings a smile to my face. :)

WEEKEND GETAWAY WITH THE CAR:

ARE WE THEEEERE YET?

You think: let's start taking baby steps. A car ride instead of a long flight, that should be doable, right? Until you're barely an hour into the trip and you'd rather walk to Paris then sit one more minute in the car with a super cranky baby. :) To avoid those feelings (or at least try), here are my favourite tips to make a long car drive with a mini as fun as possible!

PLAN YOUR TRIP DURING NAPS

That is the most strategic trip to make your road trips with a baby as pleasant as possible: plan your car trip according to his nap schedule! **Perfect when your baby's daily nap is approximately during the middle of the trip**: in those first few hours, it is easy to entertain him; once boredom sets in, it is time for a nap. And that makes those last hours all the more fun, with a rested mini and the prospect of getting there soon!

SNACKS, SNACKS, SNACKS

Strictly speaking, it is not entirely on the up and up to use snacks to keep your baby calm, but as far as I am concerned, long car trips are the exception. :) **Provide different types of bite-size snacks that do not melt, do not make a mess in small warm hands, and do not get them all hyped up** (so no fast sugars!): dried fruit, muesli, carrot sticks, apple slices.... they're all perfect. **Wrap them in small groups in opaque greaseproof paper and tie the packets with twine, turning them into small individual gifts** to provide extra entertainment with a surprise effect.

NO ELECTRONICS

Even though it may seem tempting to soothe your baby with a video on your phone or laptop, you will soon find out it actually has the opposite effect. **Moving images, bright colours and sounds stimulate your baby's brain to keep him alert and ultra-awake**, so avoid electronic entertainment as much as possible if you want to have a quiet trip. Save them for

that last hour, when all other resources have been used and the end of your trip is in sight!

TURN YOUR CAR INTO A SMALL HOUSE

The big advantage of babies is that you can easily fool them. :) **A car seat with a warm blanket, recognisable cuddly toys, and your mini's favourite lullaby are soon associated with bedtime** – just the way you want it. Just repeat a few of your evening rituals and he will be off to Neverland for a few hours...

TAKE A BREAK

The best way to soothe your baby and/or tire him out more, so he can quietly nap in the car, is to regularly make a pit stop, even if it is just for 10 minutes. **If you spot a bit of nature along the road, move to the side of the road and take a walk or have a mini picnic.** You will be surprised how much effect that bit of fresh air will have for the rest of the trip – for baby, mama and papa!

FLYING AND LONG-DISTANCE TRAVEL WITH A BABY:
HERE'S HOW

Aaah, flying with a baby: the worst fear of every new mama! In addition to the real irrational fears – the baby might get stuck *alone* in the bathroom, the plane might crash and the baby won't be able to open the mini parachute – there are also fears that effectively might come true – the baby might cry non-stop during the entire 8-hour flight, the baby might inexplicably go through his three spare outfits during the first 2 hours of the flight and arrive a sticky mess.

All of that will go through your head when you get on your first flight, full of hope. **When Gabriel was 11 months old, we travelled to Tokyo with the three of us**, his first long-distance flight (12 hours, with 1 transfer) and his first jetlag. As soon as I shared our trip on social media, I received tons of messages with the same questions: how do I manage to travel to such a faraway destination with a baby? Did I bring a nanny? (no) Wasn't I stressed out about the 12-hour flight? (super stressed) Did I manage to pack light? (absolutely not).

But phew, as it turned out: **there are loads of things that can soften the blow and make your flight and stay (reasonably) stress-free.** And bribing the people in the next seat is just one of those things! These are my ultimate tips for travelling (long-distance) with your mini!

PREPPING LIKE A PRO

DON'T FREAK OUT IN ADVANCE

As a new mama, it's something that I need to remind myself every day: **it is impossible to predict the future, and that's okay.** :) I am a control freak by nature, so when I can't control things like long-distance flights and jetlag, it drives me crazy pretty quickly. I start imagining all kinds of worst case scenarios, basically preparing myself for what might happen. Of course that stresses me out even more, plus it's completely useless and unproductive. So my first tip for travelling with a baby is simply: don't freak out in advance! So many people have gone before you, so believe in yourself – you got this.

SORT OUT YOUR PAPERWORK WELL IN ADVANCE

Babies are so cute and innocent, so you might almost forget that they also need the right paperwork to travel. :) So **check in advance** what rules and regulations apply in your destination country, and whether you need to arrange an extra visa to bring your mini.

KEEP IN MIND THAT EVERYTHING TAKES LONGER WITH A BABY

When listing all the things that babies are – cute! smiley! so cuddly! – time-efficient is most definitely not on the list. Practically everything, including travelling, takes longer with a baby. So keep that in mind with every aspect of your journey, from packing your (many) suitcases to driving to the airport and checking in. The advantage of travelling with a baby is that most services, such as checking your bags, your security check and boarding **give priority treatment to parents with a baby** – that does compensate a bit! :)

WHAT TO DO WITH YOUR STROLLER??

I consider myself to be a bit of an 'over-packer'; I always bring along too many outfits, too much make-up, souvenirs and snacks – because you never know. Add to that the fact that babies really need soooo much stuff, and I just could not picture myself getting on a plane with our mini. :) As it turns out most airline companies are pretty well prepared for this, and in case of the biggest items – stroller and/or car seat – there is such a thing as a gate-check: **permission to check them in right before entering the plane**. Gate-check items are then given a label and taken to a cargo compartment by cart, so they will be immediately available for you as soon as you land. Also make sure that you have **a fabric baby carrier in your carry-on luggage** so you can use that when transferring. Your stroller will be transported from one plane to the next with the cargo, so you will not be able to use it during the transfer.

CHOOSE A DIAPER BACKPACK INSTEAD OF A BAG

I have soooo many gorgeous bags, yet I always prefer a Pampers backpack for travelling (the one from Jem+Bea is beautiful and practical, and my personal favourite). It is just **much more convenient to have your hands free when you are on the road**, especially when you have to get in and out of taxis with a wriggly baby.

PACK A BABY EMERGENCY KIT AND A SPARE OUTFIT

Even though Gabriel had (fortunately) never been really ill before we left for Tokyo, I still brought along half a pharmacy in our bags, packing **the important things in our carry-on luggage**. I really wanted to avoid ending up with Marcio in some foreign pharmacy in Tokyo, trying to decipher Japanese prescriptions. We ended up never needing the kit, but it was reassuring to know that the option was there.

FLYING WITH A BABY

UNDER THE AGE OF 2 = FREE!

One thing is for sure: travelling with a baby will cost you precisely 0 euros more than travelling without a baby! Under the age of 2, minis travel free of charge on your lap on all flights within Europe. For intercontinental flights, you only pay a small surcharge. When you fly with two adults (for instance mama and papa) it is a good idea to **take seats that are a bit apart from each other**, funny as that may sound. That way your little baby can alternately sit on mama's and papa's lap. It has an **entertaining/soothing** effect, because it is a new environment every time! And it also ensures that the **both of you can take turns really resting**, which will definitely not happen if you sit next to each other.

NIGHT FLIGHTS (AND BABY CRIBS) ARE THE BEST

Just like it is a good idea to plan your long-distance car trips according to your baby's sleeping patterns, night flights are perfect to (hopefully) have your baby sleeping peacefully for most of the flight. **7 in the evening**

is the perfect departure time. And also do not forget to **reserve a baby crib** on the flight; super convenient to have more freedom and possibly take a nap yourself. If you do not have that option, I'd recommend booking an **extra seat** so your mini can relax in his car seat. And if you can also pack the favourite bits and pieces from your baby's evening ritual in your carry-on luggage, you can copy that *en route* (minus singing lullabies ;)). Perfect!

KEEP THOSE EARS UNBLOCKED

Although many babies cry during take-off and landing, and even though you may think this is due to the experience of the event, it is usually caused by changes in normal ear pressure. We've all had it happen: that nagging, sometimes even painful sensation in your ears caused by changing air pressure in the plane, which can lead to dizziness and reduced hearing. It helps amazingly if you make any kind of chewing movement, but since you cannot explain that to your mini, it is a great plan to **feed him during take-off or landing**. It also offers him some distraction from the inevitable commotion at the beginning and end of the flight, and mellows him out for his next nap.

NEIGHBORS AND BABIES: ENTERTAIN & DISTRACT

The biggest difference between facing car trips or flights with a baby is of course that flights also share the 'fun' with other people. **Besides the snacks for your mini, remember to bring along some additional treats for the people sitting around you**; break the ice from the start with a little gift... and I wanna bet that your neighbours will be surprisingly understanding during the umpteenth crying fit.

YOU MADE IT!

SOS JETLAG

I got a ton of questions about the best way to deal with an 11-month-old baby suffering from jetlag! This must be different for everybody, but for us this worked best: **adjusting his nap times to local time from the get-go**. If I noticed that he was still getting tired in between his naps, I let him take another short nap. It also helped tremendously to do his regular evening ritual in Tokyo: taking a bath, reading a book, giving him his last bottle and straight into bed.

CONSIDER AN APARTMENT INSTEAD OF A HOTEL IN THE CITY CENTRE

Even though we were inclined to opt for a hotel (nothing beats room service, right? :)), we were still happy that we eventually opted for a two-room apartment in the city centre. It is just **so much easier to arrange daytime naps** without having to walk on tippy toes or worrying about too much noise. And as far as the location goes: unless it is your actual intention to escape the city, it is **super convenient to stay at a location right in the city centre** to avoid long rides, and to be in reach of everything within 15 minutes. Locations like that usually cost a bit more, but they are really worth it!

RENT THE BIG THINGS AT YOUR DESTINATION

We are very satisfied with our travel crib, but we were **very happy that we could rent a crib on-site**. We didn't have to take it with us. We were in Tokyo for almost 2 weeks, so travelling light was not an option regardless. Adding a travel crib to all our baggage would have been

overkill. Given that Japanese people are usually super efficient, we did not have to think
twice about renting a crib there. It was super
easy! :)

PLAN YOUR DAYS AND HAVE FUN!
Marcio and I have always been spontaneous
travellers. But to be honest, once you have a
baby, it is much more relaxed to travel when
you have an approximate idea of your day-to-
day schedule! **Make a map of all the hot spots
you want to visit and check which ones are
clustered close together.** Based on that, the
weather and your mood, it is easy to make a
travel itinerary, including your must-do activities and favourite food spots. And most of all:
do not forget to have as much fun as possible!!
Because you can rest assured that you will
quickly forget all the hassle and fuss, while
your **good memories will last forever**. :)

MY FAV PLACES FOR MINI SHOPPING

Let's be honest: shopping for minis is FUN! :) The first three months of my pregnancy were no fun at all (constantly nauseous, but not yet able to say anything to family and friends), and **hunting down tiny shoes or mini jackets really helped soften the blow a bit**. It's just so much easier to imagine your baby when you're holding something tangible – and yes, he or she will really be that tiny at first. :)

But no matter how fun it can be to go mini shopping, it can also be pretty overwhelming to find the real gems in the *megaaaa* array of baby products. There's lots and lots of, um, less than fashionable baby clothes out there, so it's best to have some idea of where you want to go to find the cutest clothes, strollers, accessories and toys. Here's my favourite mini shops in the world's most enjoyable shopping cities!

ANTWERP

KID
Steenhouwersvest 34A, 2000 Antwerp
www.iamkid.be
A cool boutique with the best selection of clothes for infants and children, with unique limited edition brands like Caroline Bosmans and its own collection of sweatshirts. Baby swimsuits and mini sneakers are also sold here!

REWIND PLAY
Kloosterstraat 63, 2000 Antwerp
www.rewinddesign.be
Rewind Play has all sorts of cute little odds and ends for the nursery, but it's (shocking :)) mainly the clothing that makes my heart beat faster, including Hugo Loves Tiki (they have the cutest prints), Liewood (the softest basics) and Mini Rodini (too cool for school).

HET LAND VAN OOIT
Koningin Astridlaan 82C, 2550 Kontich
www.hetlandvanooit.be
The perfect shop for all your baby essentials! This is where I stocked up on my baby list, including my beloved Mima Xari stroller,

travel cot, car seat, Babyzen Yoyo stroller and so much more...

PETIT BATEAU

Huidevetterstraat 30, 2000 Antwerp
www.petit-bateau.com
Petit Bateau is one of my favourite brands for twinning – mama and mini wearing identical outfits! Twinning can sometimes be a bit too much, but never when you're wearing this brand: their famous nautical jumpers or yellow raincoats are ideal for stylish twinning. Oh, and if you really want to go full-out, papa can join in too! :)

BRUSSELS

THÉOPHILE ET PATACHOU

Louizalaan 132A, 1050 Brussels
www.theophile-patachou.com
My no. 1 spot to score the most beautiful furniture and accessories for the children's room! We opted for a neutral white theme, but if you're more of a pink-or-blue type, they'll definitely have what you're looking for.

KAT & MUIS

Oude Graanmarkt 35-37, 1000 Brussels
You'll find an amazingly broad selection of brands here that offer both mini and maxi collections, like Paul Smith, Bellerose and Stella McCartney.

PIPELETTES ET GALOPINS

Linthoutstraat 190-192, 1040 Brussels
www.pipelettes-et-galopins.com
One of the owners was originally from Sweden, and the shop reflects that: lots of simple items in soft pastels and natural fabrics. All very *lagom* :).

BONPOINT

Louizalaan 74, 1050 Brussels
www.bonpoint.com
Ideal for finding gorgeous classics with a French air. And they also have a wonderful line of perfumes and care products for minis!

PARIS

SMALLABLE

81 Rue du Cherche Midi, 75006 Paris
www.smallable.com
Following Smallable's huge online success, this family concept store opened its first brick-and-mortar location in downtown Paris. It's one of my favourite spots to find the funnest fashions, deco pieces, toys and accessories for the whole family!

LES ENFANTINES
4 Rue Vavin, 75006 Paris
www.lesenfantines.com
For all the French classics: delightful wool-
len jumpers with cotton collars, little linen
salopettes worn over a tiny shirt, and knitted
bonnets in the finest quality!

LOUIS LOUISE
83 Rue du Cherche Midi, 75006 Paris
www.louislouise.com
Another place to find the best of France, with
the most beautiful little garments in soft earth
tones and soft materials. Oh, and they have
the cutest collection of wedding outfits for the
very littlest among us!

CENTRE COMMERCIAL KIDS
22 Rue Yves Toudic, 15010 Paris
www.centrecommercial.cc
Another shop selling so much more than just
cute little clothes. My personal favourites: the
giant stuffed animals made by Big Stuffed!

LE PETIT SOUK
14 Rue de Charonne, 75011 Paris
www.lepetitsouk.fr
The perfect spot to shop for mini gifts, like
pumpkin baskets, colourful mobiles, night-
lights, birthday cards and so much more.

BONTON
85 bis Rue de Grenelle, 75007 Paris
www.bonton.fr
The very sweetest mini clothes with a touch
of France are sold here! Little *foulards* in floral
prints and socks with lace trim or preppy but-
ton-down shirts in chunky checks and white
sun hats: you'll wish they carried all these
clothes in adult sizes too...

BABY DIOR
25 Rue Royale, 75008 Paris
www.dior.com
For your very special occasions, you're sure to
find what you're looking for at Baby Dior! The
beautifully embroidered princess dresses and
perfect little shoes are ideal to cherish for a
lifetime. And thank God, you can pick out a
similar outfit in adult sizes here, to make the
picture complete. :)

GALERIES LAFAYETTE
40 Boulevard Haussmann, 75009 Paris
www.galerieslafayette.com
The iconic Galeries Lafayette also has a fantastic children's department, with the cutest
little designer collections by Boss, Burberry,
Calvin Klein, Little Marc Jacobs and more.
Everything the tiny fashionista needs!

LONDON

OLIVE LOVES ALFIE
84 Stoke Newington Church Street, N16
OAP London
www.olivelovesalfie.co.uk
No mass-produced, off-the-rack garments
here, just on-trend clothes and adorable good-
ies to make your nursery just as unique as your
mini. How about a paper maché unicorn to
hang on your wall?

LA COQUETA
5 Heath Street, NW3 6TP London
www.lacoquetakids.com
You might not expect it here, but this is a little
corner of Spain in London! Including floral
dresses, straw hats and bright white outfits for
flower girls and boys... Definitely worth a visit!

www.bobandblossom.co.uk
One word: tutus! :) They're waiting for you here in all sorts of shades, from white, grey and black to dusty rose, grass green and fuchsia. Wonderful in combination with their cool slogan T-shirts and sweatshirts! Wanna bet your mini won't want to wear anything else?

LUNA & CURIOUS

24-26 Calvert Avenue, E2 7JP London
www.lunaandcurious.com
This shop is perfect for tweaking your mini's summer wardrobe, including Izipizi sunglasses (also for mama!) and a great selection of sun hats. They also have very stylish baby bibs in sailor print or playful ruffles.

ELIAS & GRACE

158 Regent's Park Road, NW1 8XN London
www.eliasandgrace.com
Cute, clean-cut boutique with an excellent selection of international brands like Salt Water and Imps & Elfs, and they also carry their own brand: Miller, featuring all the characteristic London classics.

MAISON AUGUSTE

6 Heath Street, NW3 6TE London
www.maison-auguste.myshopify.com
The most beautiful nursery and fashion accessories for your mini! This is the place to go for fairy-tale lamps (the golden toadstools are a personal favourite!), the soft reindeer seats from Elements Optimal, and wonderfully kitschy pineapple and unicorn hair slides in every colour of the rainbow.

BOB & BLOSSOM

140 Columbia Road, E2 7RG London

NEW YORK

KITH

337 Lafayette Street, NYC, 10012
www.kith.com
This uber-cool brand relies on effortlessly playful designs, all printed on basic hoodies, T-shirts and track suits. Perfect for twinning, since they also have a super-fun collection for adults that has the same streetwear vibe.

LITTLE GIANTS

445 Albee Square, NYC, 11201
www.wearelittlegiants.com
Indubitably the coolest kids' shop in NYC! You'll find everything you need to make your mini stand out from the crowd: rompers, T-shirts and hoodies with, um, clear slogans (giant, queen bee and unruly) and the cutest caps and bottles.

where to find the most gorgeous, understated little dresses, jumpers and bloomer shorts in soft hues, in organic cotton, linen and wool. They also offer a women's collection with exactly the same vibe, perfect for stylish twinning with your mini!

HAZEL VILLAGE
510 3rd Avenue, NYC, 11215
www.hazelvillage.com
Playing dress-up is always fun, which is why this little shop in Brooklyn came up with a unique concept that's all about the outfit of... your bear! First pick your favourite animal – choices include foxes, rabbits, cats, mice and more! – and then choose the cutest handmade clothes. If you want to make it a bit more personal, you can add your mini's initials or name and pick up a matching outfit!

THE ELOISE STORE AT THE PLAZA
768 5th Avenue, NYC, 10019
www.theplazany.com
The pink suite at the NYC Plaza Hotel, inspired by Kay Thompson's book *Eloise: A Book for Precocious Grown-ups*, is the sugar-coated dream of every girl's clichéd dreams. Spend the night here, enjoy afternoon tea, or shop for the best Eloise accessories – it's all wonderful!

FLYING SQUIRREL
87 Oak Street, NYC, 11222
www.flyingsquirrelbaby.com
Every mama wrestles with this one: isn't it a shame to invest in clothing that won't be worn more than once? This little shop in Brooklyn offers an answer by carrying a super-fun selection of barely worn second-hand baby clothes, as well as its shirts and trousers made mainly by local producers.

LES PETITS CHAPELAIS
146 Sullivan Street, NYC, 10012
www.lespetitschapelais-nyc.com
Cute little boutique with a European twist in Soho, one of New York's trendiest neighbourhoods. The summer collections are especially adorable, featuring heart-melting straw hats, embroidered dresses and super-fun swimwear.

MAKIÉ
109 Thompson Street, NYC, 10012
www.makieclothier.com
One of my favourite spots to find minimalist baby clothes with a Japanese vibe! This is

ONLINE

HIGH END
www.farfetch.com
www.melijoe.com

CLASSIC
www.littlerolondon.com
www.benedita.co.uk
www.vanberen.com
www.huttelihut.dk
www.oscaretvalentine.com
www.caramel-shop.co.uk
https://yellowflamingo.fr/fr/

www.mabli.co.uk
www.sissonne.com.pt
www.tartine-et-chocolat.com
www.poeme-et-poesie.com
https://www.livlyclothing.com
www.cashmirino.com

HIP & STREETWEAR
www.orangemayonnaise.com
www.kiddinlondon.co.uk
www.sugarpaperblue.com
www.superism.co
www.nununuworld.com
www.mylittlecozmo.com
http://www.paperplainbrand.com
www.thekidssupply.com
www.hausofjr.com
www.loud-apparel.com
www.someday-soon.com
www.zombiedash.pl
www.unauthorized.dk
www.beauloves.co.uk
www.carbonsoldier.com
www.tinycottons.com
www.noe-zoe.com
www.carolinebosmans.com

ECO-FRIENDLY & ONE-OF-A-KIND
www.organic-zoo.com
www.naturebaby.eu
www.lespetitsbios.fr
www.rootswings.dk
www.wovenplay.com
www.liewood.com
www.kukukid.com
www.gray-label.com
www.woollywonderknits.co.uk
www.marlonandlittlefriends.com
www.gogentlynation.com
www.donsje.com

In closing

How do you end a book that's sooooo personal? A book where you've shared one of the most precious parts of your life with the rest of the world, because you hope that it can at least make other mamas feel: **you're not alone**. :) People asked quite a lot of questions when I announced my first pregnancy. How did I expect to fit the baby into my hectic lifestyle? How would the fashion industry respond to a sometimes less-than-glamorous mini-addition to our family? How would we manage with all that travel, and was it irresponsible to take along a baby? All those questions occasionally felt pretty weird, because if I knew one thing for sure, it was this: I'll figure it out. The truth is: **a baby doesn't necessarily have to be a limiting factor in your life**; it can also just be **fun**. Sharing the big news with your family, styling your baby bump, hunting down those first tiny baby clothes, figuring out how to fake that pregnancy glow if it doesn't appear naturally, picking the name and the birth announcements, preparing the nursery, going on your babymoon, and then packing your hospital delivery bag in those nerve-wracking last few weeks. But also: coping with so many new emotions, learning how to truly take it easier, asking yourself what kind of mama you want to be, and then trying to incorporate that tiny new little person into your life as well as possible. And yep, that means putting together the perfect diaper bag and hunting down the cutest mama-and-baby twinning outfits, just as much as it means coming up with smart tricks to cope with all those short nights, and pulling out all the stops to make great memories for your very first Christmas, Easter, Mother's Day, Father's Day, summer holiday and Halloween. Doesn't sound so bad, does it?

And remember, the most important thing to keep in mind as a new mama, after carrying your mini with you for months inside your own body, bringing him into the world, and trying every day from then on to make him the happiest human ever: no matter how many opinions, well-meaning tips and tricks, or photos of the 'perfect mama' you see, **you should just do what feels right for you**. Nothing is more personal than being a mama, and no one knows what's good for your baby better than you do.
Mama knows best, and that's the truth.

Love,
Sofie

Colophon

www.lannoo.com

Register on our website to receive regular newsletters with information on new books and interesting, exclusive offers.

Text & Editing
Sofie Valkiers

Photography
Marcio Bastos

Translation
Joy Phillips

Book Design
Leen Depooter - quod. voor de vorm.

If you have comments or questions, please contact our editing department at redactielifestyle@lannoo.com

© Uitgeverij Lannoo nv, Tielt, 2018
D/2018/45/546 – NUR 450/452
ISBN: 978 94 014 5691 3